GET
YOUR
BUSINESS
ONLINE
NOW!

GET YOUR BUSINESS ONLINE

NOW!

Todd Alexander
Australia's leading online expert

hachette
AUSTRALIA

hachette
AUSTRALIA

Published in Australia and New Zealand in 2012
by Hachette Australia
(an imprint of Hachette Australia Pty Limited)
Level 17, 207 Kent Street, Sydney NSW 2000
www.hachette.com.au

10 9 8 7 6 5 4 3 2 1

Copyright © Todd Alexander 2012

National Library of Australia
Cataloguing-in-Publication data

Alexander, Todd
Get your business online – now / Todd Alexander.

978 0 7336 2898 6 (pbk.)

Electronic commerce – Australia.
Small business – Australia – Computer network resources.

381.142

Cover design by Xou Creative
Text design by Shaun Jury, Publications Designs
Typeset in Proforma and FF Din by Shaun Jury, Publications Designs
Printed in Australia by Griffin Press, Adelaide, an Accredited ISO AS/NZS 4001:2004
Environmental Management Systems printer

The paper this book is printed on is certified against the
Forest Stewardship Council® Standards. Griffin Press holds
FSC chain of custody certification SGS-COC-005088. FSC
promotes environmentally responsible, socially beneficial
and economically viable management of the world's
forests.

Contents

Introduction

As a business owner in Australia you've probably been asking yourself for some time whether your business needs to be online. If you're already online, you probably ask yourself how much you need to spend to optimise your online presence and how best to get people to buy from you online. Gone are the days of questioning whether online is appropriate for your business because whether you're a retailer, service provider, wholesaler or other business, you will more than likely be feeling the pinch of today's economic environment.

Do I Need to be Online?

Getting online, and doing it effectively, is mandatory for all Australian businesses. Here's why . . .

Running your own Business is Getting Tougher

Three recent events have significantly impacted Australian business owners' ability to maintain profitability.

1. Dealing with the global financial crisis (GFC) affected most businesses negatively and while Australia

narrowly missed slumping into full-blown recession, the GFC had a significant impact on consumer confidence. By March 2011, consumer confidence had fallen to a new nine-month low. Retailers were among the hardest hit, with growth month after month generally reported as being flat at best.

2. Partway through 2011, however, confidence began to increase, producing a direct impact on the value of the Australian dollar. As the Australian dollar reached, then exceeded, parity with the US dollar, Australian consumers were given a boost – but this came in the form of renewed confidence in spending the Australian dollar offshore. Forrester Research[1] estimates that around 25 per cent of all online spending, for example, is to overseas retailers.

3. The growth of the internet and its penetration into the Australian household means around 80 per cent of the population are internet users, according to Forrester. The more people who use the internet, the easier it becomes for them to compare prices.

Is Online a Viable Channel to Help me Grow my Business?

This was the question a lot of Australian business owners began asking themselves in 2010 and 2011. As retailers went to the media and government complaining about the internet's large negative impact on their business, the media responded by comparing online with traditional bricks-and-mortar stores. The comparison ultimately highlighted the considerable savings available online for Australian consumers. Not only did this bring Australian retailers into the eCommerce debate more vocally than ever before, it also improved consumer awareness of the benefits of online shopping. But online is much more than retail – it also represents opportunities for wholesalers, service providers, professionals and any business owner in Australia to find new customers.

The internet is rapidly changing the way Australians communicate, learn, have fun and shop. There is tremendous growth predicted for Australian eCommerce, and in order to compete, businesses must adapt by integrating online into their multi-channel strategies.

Deborah Sharkey, Vice President and Managing Director, eBay Australia and New Zealand Pty Ltd

Let's look at two reasons why online is one answer to helping grow your business.

eCommerce in Australia is Worth $34 Billion Dollars Annually

It is not only retailers who are beginning to appreciate the possibility that online will help grow any business, rather than cannibalising existing sales. Forrester Research reports that 80 per cent of all Australians (or more than 14 million) over the age of 16 are online, and of these, 54 per cent (or 9.7 million) purchase items over the internet. The total amount spent by Australians online in 2012 is forecast by Forrester to reach over $34 *billion*, with an annual growth rate of 12.6 per cent. This growth is in stark contrast to bricks-and-mortar retail, which is more or less flat. But this number only represents the dollars processed via online transactions – every day, millions of customers go online to research products and services.

> There is no doubt retailers need to respond to current consumer demand by including online eCommerce offerings in their business mix.
> *Russell Zimmerman, Executive Director,*
> *Australian Retailers Association*

A conservative estimate for the number of times Australians will conduct an internet search in 2012 is around *80 billion*[2]. That equates to 220 million searches every single day. Of these billions of search terms entered into Australian search engines each year, how many relate to your business? <u>If your customers can't find you online, chances are they will easily find one of your competitors</u>. Not only could you be losing existing customers, you could also be missing out on tapping into a whole new set of customers.

How are People Finding you Today?

Take a moment to think about how your customers are finding you today. It is likely to be a combination of the following:

- Word of mouth
- Passing trade
- Offline media advertising – television, radio or print
- Offline directories – *Yellow* and *White Pages*, industry lists, etc.
- Online directories – search engines
- Other online – advertising, trading platforms

There may be other ways your customers are finding you but unless you ask, you may never get the full picture. Without a clear idea of where your customers look for you, you will have little chance of spending your marketing budget effectively. <u>The point of this is to ask your customers, as often as possible, how they heard about you.</u>

Train your staff to ask them what they are looking for, if they've conducted any research about the item, if they use the internet … Your customers are an irreplaceable source of information that can help you improve your business's sales and profits. Only when you start hearing it from your customers directly will you begin to appreciate the true opportunity that online represents for your business.

How do I get my Business Online?

The writing is very clearly on the wall for Australian businesses and to ignore it will probably result in poor business growth, or perhaps zero or negative growth. Your customers *are* online and they want to see you there, too. The great news is that getting online doesn't have to cost you a fortune. In fact, you can begin your online expansion without even having a website, and I will show you how.

> eCommerce is increasingly embedded deep into the lives of more and more consumers. A change like this comes along once a generation; every entrepreneur and retailer needs to have a very clear perspective on how to respond to the internet's challenges and opportunities.
> *Simon Smith, Director, Quantium Online*

I've spent over ten years helping Australian businesses get online successfully. Throughout this book, I will show you a variety of options for getting your business online, covering everything you need to know and, more importantly, helping you prioritise which options are the most cost-effective for your business.

In the chapters of this book you will discover how to:

- Get online without a website
- Create an effective website
- Accept payments online
- Pack and send your goods/deliver your service – the logistics of eCommerce
- Build a website that drives traffic from search engines free of charge
- Use advertising to drive traffic to your website
- Use social media sites such as Facebook in your online business
- Use mobile retail in eCommerce
- Provide online customer support – how is it different?

Throughout the book, I will include some examples of businesses that have effective eCommerce strategies so you can pick the best of the best to create your own solution. I'll speak to some of Australia's best eCommerce experts and share their advice with you. I will be giving you fun and interactive homework to complete and all of this will culminate, most importantly, in a prioritised eCommerce action plan for your business.

By the end of this book, you will be able to launch an immediate, successful and cost-effective online strategy that will help the growth of your business.

Despite popular arguments, Australian online commerce is alive and well and growing at more than 10 per cent per annum. In the majority of cases, it is small businesses that are driving this growth. With close to 9 million Australians using the internet to buy goods and services, this number will only grow as Australia's access to broadband internet services improves. PayPal's research shows that the majority of Australian consumers prefer to 'Buy Aussie'; there are huge opportunities for Australian businesses to dive into the world of online commerce and to reap success by reaching new customers and increasing their revenue streams.

Frerk-Malte Feller, former Managing Director, PayPal Australia

Homework:

Conduct an internet search on your business name. Make a note of whether it appeared at all and if so, what page and position of the search results you appeared on. Who appeared above or near you?

Next, conduct an internet search for the kind of products or services your business sells. Where are you now? Who performs better than you?

1
Third Party Websites

Getting online without having a website – part one

WHAT THIS CHAPTER WILL COVER

- Sell to online customers without having a website

- Outsource all components of the sale to a third party – marketing, payments and logistics

- Sell large volumes of discounted products and services quickly

- The dangers of not 'owning' your customers' transactions

- Protect your brand's value by clearing excess stock or discounting your service to a restricted number of consumers for a limited time

- Attract new customers to your products or service

You Don't Have to Have a Website to get Online

Let me start by being very clear: *not* having a website cannot be your entire long-term eCommerce strategy. It is strongly recommended that every business has its own website because websites are the cornerstone of every eCommerce strategy. Not having a website is like having a business without a name and hoping that customers find you by sheer chance.

Make Online Sales Without 'Owning' the Customer

Be aware that some online options allow you to make the sale but hand over ownership of the customer: you are effectively outsourcing all components of the sale to a third party. That third party retains your customers' contact details, shopping preferences and payment information and therefore retains the ability to make further communications and develop a relationship with that customer. It goes without saying that this is a restricted entry into eCommerce and one that is not sustainable over a long period of time. The aim of any effective eCommerce strategy should be to attract – and retain – new and existing customers because only then can you build loyalty to your business and create cost-effective online marketing campaigns.

Short-term Benefits of Utilising Third Party Sites

If you do not currently have a website, or are finding it difficult to drive traffic to your website, there is a small number of popular options for you to attract customers, and they're available right now. Every year or so, a brand-new fad sweeps through the online world. It arguably began with auctions around 15 years ago but lately, three types of sites have driven online consumers into frenzied buying activity. Collectively, these are known as group-buying sites. In 2011, a study from Telsyte[3] reported that the group-buying market would reach $400 million and was experiencing quarter-on-quarter growth of 72 per cent.

Coupon Sites ✓

Also known as Group Buy or Groupon (named after the most successful US operator), coupon sites have emerged over the past 12 months or so as the most exciting and popular way for consumers to find great deals on products and experiences online. Here's how they work:

- Consumers subscribe to a coupon site of their choice (most consumers subscribe to multiple sites).
- Businesses provide a large discount to site subscribers, offering their goods or service at the discount rate for one day, or one week only, or offering a limited number until the quantity runs out.
- Consumers receive daily or weekly emails or mobile alerts outlining deals in their local area.

- Together, buyers must usually agree to purchase a combined minimum quantity. Only then will the offer become active.
- The coupon site company takes a percentage of your turnover on the special deal and sends customers a code, coupon or other identifier so you can grant them access to the special offer.

In practice, let's say I own a bar in Sydney's CBD. A coupon site salesperson will visit me, or else I can contact the site directly, and between us we agree a special deal for that site's subscribers – something like 75 per cent off cocktails for three hours one night. The site host then sends an email to all their subscribers alerting them to my deal. Most of these sites work on minimum volume, and will drive significant amounts of traffic to my bar. Large subscriber bases mean that my offer will go to considerably more people than I could manage via my own marketing network. While 75 per cent off cocktails sounds like an incredible deal to customers, I know my cost price of cocktails is 25 per cent, so I will not lose money on this deal. In this case, I hope that people will like my bar so much that they stay beyond the three hours and end up ordering full-priced drinks, or buy food while they are there, or come back another time and pay full price for their drinks, or they tell their friends about my bar and I get more customers that way. It's a classic retail strategy (known as a loss leader) that generally works very well.

Most coupon sites in Australia operate in more or less the same way. While they are reluctant to publicise their exact subscriber numbers, be sure to ask how big their subscriber base is before you commit to providing a deal. At the time of writing, the five sites that attract the most visitors in Australia are:

1. **Cudo** (www.cudo.com.au) A joint venture between Microsoft and Nine Entertainment, Cudo attracts over 750 000 unique Australian visitors each month.

2. **Spreets** (www.spreets.com.au) Working in conjunction with Yahoo!7, Spreets was launched in February of 2010. It attracts around 650 000 Australians each month.

3. **Scoopon** (www.scoopon.com.au) James Packer's Consolidated Press Holdings recently made $80 million worth of investments in this and other websites. It attracts around 580 000 Australians each month.

4. **Living Social** (www.livingsocial.com) With headquarters based in the US, the company began in July 2009 and now appears in 21 countries and, according to Wikipedia, is valued at about US$3 billion. It attracts around 560 000 Australians each month.

5. **Groupon Inc** (www.groupon.com.au) Another US-based company, Wikipedia reports that it was preparing for a US$25 billion initial public offering (IPO) in 2011 and Google famously missed out on acquiring it for a reported $6 billion. It attracts around 530 000 Australians each month.

Most of these sites have a link that says something like 'for businesses' or 'feature your business' and the link will take you to directions on how to supply their customers with special offers.

There are some things you need to be aware of before deciding to partner with one of these sites. In a very insightful post published on www.techcrunch.com,[4] the author suggested the following factors helped business owners decide whether participating in a daily deal site would be successful or not:

- Make sure you negotiate a deal with the site that remains profitable for your business.
- Have systems in place to keep track of who redeems the voucher, and how much they spend (if possible, try to track future spend of the customer as well).
- Ensure you have a clear understanding of the economics involved – How many customers are you expecting? How much of a discount are you offering? What is your cost structure? Etc.

One of the business owners I spoke to felt that the sales teams from the coupon sites often do not have a lot of online knowledge or experience so he was reluctant to take their advice without doing significant research himself. Always do your homework thoroughly before agreeing to discount your products, and have an accurate business plan calculated to help ensure you will make money from the overall experience, not just give your product away to hungry online bargain hunters with little, or no, benefit to your business.

Who's doing it well?

- Food and accommodation companies were the first to jump on to the latest eCommerce trend as it allowed them to gauge how much online demand there was for their products.
- Health and beauty businesses also frequently offer services at a greatly reduced rate; most are initial consultations on a service that requires ongoing treatment to be entirely successful. By giving discounts on the first one to three treatments, the business hopes to secure the customer for the full course of treatments.

Private Shopping Clubs

Particularly strong at fashion sales, private shopping clubs began in Europe a few years ago and soon swept through the online world. Some of the best fashion brands in the world have allowed their products to be discounted up to 80 per cent off retail by offering their end-of-line or overstock items to private shopping clubs. This option is generally limited to manufacturers or wholesalers of products, but check with each site to see which categories they specialise in, or what types of businesses they are sourcing products from.

Here's how private shopping clubs work:

- Buyers sign up to be a member of a shopping club purporting to be 'private' or 'exclusive'. In reality, most will accept anyone as a member or, as a minimum, ask for a friend to refer you.

- Product suppliers provide their unwanted stock at an incredibly reduced rate to clear inventory and free up valuable storage or instore space. This is done at an agreed reduction off recommended retail price, a set flat rate or via a revenue share agreement where the supplier and the club host split the sale price.

- Often the goods are provided to the private shopping club host on consignment, that is, the club does not purchase any items up front, but waits to see how many are wanted by its members before confirming an order with the supplier.

- Club members receive an email offering a range of items at reduced prices for a strictly limited time.

- At the close of the sale, the supplier sends the items to the club's warehouse and they are then dispatched to buyers.

- Buyers generally have to wait two to four weeks to receive their products but accept this, given the discount they receive.

Most shopping clubs work best for popular, brand-name items. Businesses protective of their brand's 'value' do not like to have masses of product on sale to the general public or in retail stores so prefer to use private clubs to restrict awareness and quantities. It is deemed to be less damaging to the brand's reputation among consumers.

At the time of writing, the three sites that attract the most visitors in Australia are:

1. **Ozsale** (www.ozsale.com.au) Founded in 2007, Australia's leading private sales club attracts around 720 000 Australians each month. It recently received a $14 million investment from Insight Venture Partners (who also invested in Twitter).

2. **brandsExclusive** (www.brandsexclusive.com.au) Australian-based private sales club staffed by experienced retailers and eCommerce professionals attracting nearly 600 000 Australians each month.

3. **buyinvite** (www.buyinvite.com.au) This site has over one million Australian members (traffic figures not available).

As with coupon sites, make sure you shop around and weigh up which club is best for your products. Look for clubs that buy products outright so you do not have to worry about being left with completely unmoveable stock, that is, stock that won't even sell at up to 80 per cent off retail price. Another tip is to find eBay's top sellers in your category (see Chapter Two) and ask them if they are interested in expanding their range to include your products; most eBay sellers are hungry for more stock, especially well-priced branded stock from Australian manufacturers and wholesalers.

Who's doing it well?

- Premium Australian fashion brands were fast to utilise these sites to clear excess inventory (often styles or sizes that did not sell well at retail) from warehouses. This inventory costs more to store than it does to sell at a rate of up to 75 per cent off. Fashion brands are particularly protective of their brand value and use private clubs to protect it by discounting only a selected range to the club's members for a strictly limited time.
- Electronics manufacturers have recently added their products to the mix, giving private club members more to choose from than just fashion.

Deals Sites

Basically wholesalers or 'middlemen', deals sites offer limited (most are daily) deals to their customers on a first come, first served basis. The deal ends when all quantities are exhausted, or at the end of the advertised period. Most will handle the entire end-to-end experience for you, while eBay works with its sellers to promote deals but the seller is responsible for order fulfilment.

At the time of writing, the five sites that attract the most visitors in Australia are:

1. **eBay** (www.eBay.com.au) eBay recently launched two fresh initiatives – Deals (deals.ebay.com.au) and weekly Group Deals (groupdeals.ebay.com.au). eBay works with its sellers to hunt for the best products at the best prices and offers a restricted number for sale for a limited time. Look for the largest sellers in your category and ask if they are interested in selling your products on eBay. Attracts 5.4 million Australians to its site each month.

2. **Catch of the Day** (www.catchoftheday.com.au) A former eBay seller, Catch of the Day has grown in popularity over recent months and now attracts just over one million Australians each month.

3. **DealsDirect** (www.dealsdirect.com.au) Another eBay seller who grew to create one of Australia's largest e-tailers, DealsDirect sells a large range of products at heavily discounted prices. Recently, James Packer's private equity firm, Ellerston Capital, invested in the company. Attracts around 900 000 Australians each month.

> I think it was Shakespeare who once wrote,
> 'There is nothing new under the sun', and in
> many ways, despite the pioneering digital age
> we all find ourselves in, I think he was right. A
> great customer experience has always been
> the key driver to retail success. And always
> will be.
> *Paul Greenberg, Executive Chairman,*
> *DealsDirect Group*

4. **Grays Online** (www.graysonline.com.au)
   A predominantly auction-based website that starts
   all auctions at $9 and charges buyers an additional
   premium for successful bids. Grays Online has
   garnered a reputation for offering unbeatable deals on
   seconds in the appliances and electronics categories,
   and is a leader in the wine category. Attracts over
   650 000 Australians each month.
5. **OO** (www.oo.com.au) This site began selling on eBay
   then launched OO, which specialises in electronics and
   homewares. Frequently experiments with sales and
   deals, attracting around 600 000 Australians each
   month.

Who's doing it well?

- Electronics and gadgets are the most common item featured on deals sites. Often the site sources a complete range of products from a manufacturer or supplier and chooses which of the range to heavily discount and feature in sales.
- eBay sellers often provide free postage as an additional buyer incentive, while sites such as DealsDirect frequently offer free delivery if buyers pay with PayPal.

Homework:

Sign up to three third party deal sites (a combination of group buys, coupons and deals sites). Take note of the kinds of products or services that were on sale, the price you paid and the overall experience offered by the third party. Assess whether your business could utilise these sites as an entry point into eCommerce, or as a way to expand your website's awareness. What margin do you have on your products or services, and how far can you discount and still make profit?

CHAPTER SUMMARY

- You appreciate that third party deals and sales sites can provide a convenient entry point into eCommerce.

- Third party sites often entail outsourcing the end-to-end experience, which limits the amount of control you have.

- By not owning the transaction, you may be missing out on an opportunity to secure repeat purchases or communicate with your buyers in the future.

- You understand which sites attract the most visitors each month and their specialty categories, and have drawn up a shortlist that might be utilised by your business.

2
Online Marketplaces

Getting online without having a website – part two

WHAT THIS CHAPTER WILL COVER

- What online marketplaces are and which ones are the most popular
- How online marketplaces work
- The pros and cons of online marketplaces
- How sellers within the marketplace can remain competitive
- A list of online marketplaces to consider for your business
- Tips for becoming a marketplace seller

What are Online Marketplaces?

Online marketplaces provide a venue for you to sell your goods or services to buyers. Both you and the buyer need to be registered members of the marketplace and, once registered, you are more or less free to sell almost anything. To compare to the offline world, they play a similar role to that of landlord: you pay rent or a percentage of your sales in return for the ability to open your shop in their shopping centre. They drive traffic (customers) to the site and once there, you attract customers to your services or products and then transact directly with the customer.

You Must Play by the Rules

All marketplaces have their own rules and policies, and it is crucial to fully understand these, and the implications of breaking them. When you register, make sure you read the user agreement in its entirety, and understand it completely. Then, do your research on the site and pay particular attention to rules and policies that may apply to your business, or the products or services that you intend to sell. The last position you want to find yourself in is to be fully reliant on a marketplace for the health of your business, only to find that you are suspended for breaking one of its rules. Marketplaces play an impartial role in the sale of goods and services, that is, they tend to take limited responsibility for the sale and therefore apply their rules strictly and stringently.

How Marketplaces Work

- Buyers and sellers register to participate in the marketplace.

- The marketplace provides the platform, that is, the search functionality, (often) the shopping cart, the checkout, and sometimes the payment mechanism.
- You are responsible for fulfilling the sale, that is, collecting payment and distributing your products to buyers, or providing the service.
- You pay the marketplace a percentage of the sale, and sometimes other upfront costs.
- The marketplace is responsible for driving traffic to the site, maintaining general marketing programs and encouraging repeat activity.
- Some marketplaces allow you to retain the customer, others make it more difficult for you to communicate with your customers directly.
- Often the marketplace provides your business with the opportunity to have a website within the website, that is, all of your products merchandised on one page, with a unique URL (website address).

In practice, let's say I have a line of fashion items to sell. I register as a seller on the marketplace and agree to abide by its user agreement. I access the site's listing process either directly, or by providing a list of products via an automated feed that accesses the site's API (application programming interface – web code that allows one system to interact with another). Some sites require an upfront (or listing) fee, or charge for optional marketing extras to help my product stand out from the crowd. I set the price I want for the item, how long it will be available for sale, and the quantity for sale. I provide all product information, a photograph, and payment and postage information (if applicable) according to my own terms of trade. The marketplace then displays my product for sale to its buyers – most are driven by a sophisticated search engine that reads product titles and shows buyers the most relevant products to the keywords they have entered. If the buyer chooses to purchase my item, I enter into a sales agreement with the buyer directly. The buyer usually pays me via a checkout on the site; I collect payment and then send the buyer my products. The marketplace deducts a percentage from the sale.

The Transparency of Marketplaces

One of the greatest benefits of using a marketplace is also potentially one of its greatest challenges to the profitability of your business. All products are publicly visible at all times, which means your products are heavily scrutinised not only by buyers, but also by your competition. This is the greatest challenge of being online – your buyers can compare you to your competitors with a few clicks of a mouse. But this transparency can also work in your favour as you, in turn, get to appreciate the full experience offered by your competitors. When using marketplaces, consider the following competitive assessment criteria before sending your products online:

- Price – Anywhere your products can be viewed next to identical products from competitors, consumers will generally look to price as the first differentiator. While price may not always be the only factor in determining whether a customer purchases from you or someone else, if your pricing is considerably higher than your competitors', it's likely you will erode your customer base. Similarly, be wary of being the price leader in a category; sometimes buyers will read into the cheapest price that the product is not genuine, the service is not high quality, or your customer service is substandard.

- Postage costs – Wherever possible, if you need to send your products to buyers, offer free postage. Consumers are increasingly demanding it, and more online retailers are providing it. Some businesses incorporate the cost of postage into the item price, and still attract more buyers than those with a cheaper item and an additional charge for postage. Traditionally, buyers dislike being 'surprised' by what they see as additional or hidden costs. Manage your buyers' expectations and clearly outline one total cost.

- Postage and payment services – Make sure you remain competitive with the types of postage and payment services you offer/accept. Don't overwhelm your buyers with too much choice, but provide the most popular options for your type of goods or services.

- Item details – When using marketplaces, often the temptation is to provide brief descriptions of what is for sale. This is a common mistake. Always employ your business's branding wherever possible, and a clear, comprehensive and appealing display of the product or service.

- Customer service – Often buyers will choose to buy from the marketplace seller who provides the best service. This improves buyer confidence and, sometimes, buyers will choose to pay more for an item when they trust the seller above others. Consider providing cost-free returns if the buyer is unsatisfied for any reason, guarantees or warranties, or 24-hour customer service including telephone or live chat support (for more information see Chapter Nine).
- Overall experience – Do everything in your power to provide your products or services as part of an unbeatable overall buyer experience. Your products should be very well packaged to ensure safe delivery and have clear branding. Consider including free add-on products or product samples, marketing materials to direct buyers back to you (whether that be on the marketplace, your own website, or your physical business), and a nice thank you note is always well received.

Remember, buyers at an online marketplace are purchasing from someone they have never met. You should create an online experience to rival the best possible in-person experience. There are no sales people in the flow of the sale, no attendants to thank them for their purchase and wish them a good day and no glossy bag to hold their items. If you provide these types of nice-to-have experiences virtually, you will fast stand out from the millions of online sellers, help drive repeat purchases from your buyers and spread positive word of mouth.

Customer Feedback on Online Marketplaces

Above, I've outlined ways to help keep your buyers happy. The danger of not clearly setting your buyers' expectations, then meeting or exceeding them, is that some marketplaces provide a platform for buyers to comment on your performance. Even if you are not using a marketplace, businesses today need to be aware that in seconds, a disgruntled buyer can email, tweet, post to Facebook or blog about you and these can, in rare cases, have a devastating impact on your business. In yesteryear, a customer could yell and scream on your business's premises and the impact was generally limited to only those who were within earshot at the time. Today, there is an entire industry centred around public praise and criticism of business. It's impossible to avoid, and impossible to please all consumers, but in the case of online marketplaces, be fast to respond to any negative sentiment.

Marketplaces to Consider for your Business

Why should you consider marketplaces at all, as opposed to driving traffic to your own website? The simple answer is the quality of traffic that most marketplaces attract. The vast majority of marketplace visitors are in the market to buy a specific item. Marketplaces attract buyers; search engines attract buyers, but they also attract people wanting to have fun, research, communicate, gamble, travel ... and the list goes on. By definition, therefore, you might argue that marketplaces are the more cost-effective way to show buyers your products or services.

In the following pages I outline many of the most important marketplaces that may be applicable to your business. It's unlikely that any business will have the resources or capacity to use every single one of these and you should strictly prioritise which one or two make the most sense for your business. To help you consider which is best for you, ask yourself:

- Does it accept business listings in my category? Is there a market for my product on the site and can I compete with existing sellers' prices and service?
- How many potential buyers does the site attract each month?
- How much does it cost to list, and sell, on the site?
- How easy is it to list on the site, and what other services (logistics, data, customer service and marketing) does the site offer?
- Will I be able to retain my own branding and do I own the customer?
- What are the site's rules and policies; can I obey them and what happens if I accidentally break one of them?

In order of most popular – as measured by monthly Australian online visitors to the site at the time of writing – below is a list of the marketplaces you should consider for your business.

eBay (www.ebay.com.au)

Here's something you may not know about eBay: it's no longer the second-hand auction marketplace it first was. You may have seen some of its marketing campaigns recently, which deliberately position eBay as a cheaper alternative to retail. In fact, over 78 per cent of all items available on the site are fixed price ('buy it now', not auction), and the vast majority of these are brand-new items for sale from business sellers. Over 12 years old, today eBay is a household brand name in Australia and often the first port of call for anyone looking to buy a product online. eBay has become synonymous with great deals and an enormous range and while new and fixed price might be the vast majority of eBay's sales today, you can still find the world's largest selection of second-hand and rare or collectable items there, too.

eBay's top 2000 Australian businesses were growing at an astonishing rate of 38 per cent (year over year), which is in stark contrast to the generally flat rate of growth of traditional retail in Australia. Refer to my basic guide *How to Use eBay & PayPal* or the more advanced guide *How to Make Money on eBay* for more detailed instructions on launching your eBay business, but below are some key considerations.

eBay partners with thousands of Australian businesses and enables them to compete without expensive rent or marketing overheads, allowing them to reach the six million Australians who visit eBay each month.

Deborah Sharkey, Vice President and Managing Director, eBay Australia and New Zealand Pty Ltd

Why Consider Using eBay?

- It's Australia's most popular online marketplace, which attracts around six million Australians each month.
- eBay will never compete with its sellers in its own marketplace.
- The site has among the most competitive rates available with an option for zero upfront listings fees and a maximum fee rate of 7.9 per cent – for more expensive items, amounts above $75 are charged a rate as low as 3.5 per cent.
- It is a global marketplace that offers your products for sale to all corners of the world for no extra cost.
- eBay stores give your business its own URL (or website address) and allow you to maintain your individual branding.

- Note that eBay is predominantly a hard-goods website and though you can list services and accommodation on the site, these are not the most popular categories for buyers.

- eBay's two mobile apps, one for site-wide search, the other specifically for use in finding great deals (available at the iTunes store), mean your products will be available via mobile and can be purchased anytime, anywhere without you having to invest in mobile development. For a complete list of eBay mobile apps including Android, BlackBerry and Windows, visit http://pages2.ebay.com.au/mobile.

How to Use eBay – Top Tips

1. Be sure to choose a username that clearly reflects your business. Your exact business name may already be taken by someone else, so you may need a variation but be sure to stay as close as possible to your ideal name. If you have an existing eBay account, change its username to make it consistent with your business name.

2. Become a buyer first. Buy five to ten items to get a better understanding of how the site works. Buy from your eBay competitors to gauge how well they perform in the areas of customer service and order fulfilment. Is there anything you can learn from them, and do better than them?

3. Do your research. On eBay, conduct completed item searches for products and categories you intend selling. This will highlight recent sales, average prices, success rate, best performing sellers, etc. However, if you want to make your life easier, subscribe to Terapeak (www.terapeak.com), an independent eBay research tool that looks back over the past to summarise this information for you. It can tell you complete category sales, sell-through rates, average prices, etc. It should be every new seller's starting point on eBay to help decide what products to sell, and at what price points.

4. Open an eBay store. Not only are the fees charged to eBay's store owners generally the lowest on the site, but they provide you with the ability to create your own website within eBay, with your own URL. The store aggregates all your products for sale in one place so your buyers can more easily choose from your entire range. Stores also come with a range of marketing tools and reporting that helps you optimise your business.

5. Employ consistent branding. Your eBay username, store name, store design and listing template design should all be consistent and heavily branded with your business's logo, colours and other identifiers. You will need to have your eBay store and listing templates professionally designed, but the investment is well worth it.

6. Use eBay or third party listing tools. To list your inventory on eBay manually – that is, filling in the sell form for every single product – requires an enormous time investment. You can streamline your business effectively by utilising one of the several tools available to make it faster and easier to list and to manage your inventory and the after sales process. Some of these are covered in Chapter Five, others can be found by conducting an internet search. eBay's own tool, Selling Manager Pro, is an intermediate tool that is adequate for businesses listing up to 500–1000 items on eBay. More sophisticated tools and stand-alone services can help you efficiently list up to millions of items.

7. Accept PayPal. The vast majority of eBay buyers tend to use PayPal, the payment mechanism owned by eBay. More about PayPal is covered in Chapter Four.

8. Optimise for Best Match. eBay uses a default search algorithm it calls Best Match. There are four main ways to help improve the position of your products within search results:

   a. Popularity, as measured by recent sales and clicks through to your product's listing. The more you sell, the more popular your product is rated. By default, price tends to be the deciding factor in popularity on eBay so if you are not competitively priced, it's unlikely you will appear at the top of search results. To maximise the number of sales you can have over a given time period, you should also list your items in 30-day duration, fixed-price listings ('buy it now', not auction) and include a high quantity of items in each listing.

b. Seller performance – On eBay, there are two ways that buyers can rate you: feedback and detailed seller ratings. Ensure you provide outstanding (world-class) service to all of your eBay customers by setting clear expectations then exceeding them. Communicate quickly and effectively, post the item as soon as you receive payment, offer free postage. If something does go wrong, do everything in your power to make the buyer happy by offering refunds and exchanges and proactively taking control of the situation to provide the best possible solution. Also, ensure you abide by eBay's policies and pay your bill on time.

c. Relevance – Employ the most relevant keywords in your item title. Ensure you list your item in the correct product category.

d. Free shipping – Wherever possible, offer your buyers a free shipping method.

9. List internationally – Why not expand your potential buyer base from 6 million Australians to the more than 90 million people who use eBay globally? It costs nothing extra to have your items appear on other eBay sites around the world. Make sure you clearly outline postage costs to each country.

10. Teach yourself something new about the site every single week. I encourage every eBay seller I speak to to set aside one hour each week to learn a new area of the site. I have often said that eBay requires a 10 000 page user manual and there is hardly anyone who would have the time to understand every single corner of the site. However, eBay is packed with time- and cost-cutting tools and tips and if you take the time to learn more of them, you will undoubtedly improve the performance of your business by reducing time and labour overheads, thereby increasing overall profit.

11. Speak to eBay about participating in their Big Deal and other sales to drive instant traffic to your eBay listings.

12. Aim for eBay Top Rated Seller (eTRS) status, which you can receive if you have consistently high service standards. eTRS sellers receive additional search exposure and a logo highlighting their performance to buyers.

Who's doing it well?

- eBay's success was built by sellers who generally did not have existing businesses. These were mums and dads who taught themselves how to use the site, and built up their own businesses, usually working from home or their garage.
- As eBay evolved, more retailers have begun to utilise the site as a complementary sales channel to their existing websites or bricks-and-mortar stores.
- DealsDirect and OO used eBay before launching their own highly successful websites and still use eBay today.
- Book retailers such as The Nile, Booktopia, Treeet and Borders are among the more recognisable bookselling brands on eBay.
- After books, fashion retailers were the second major retail category to embrace the site en masse. Current sellers on the site include: Zanerobe, Witchery, Seafolly, Jigsaw, Marcs and many others.

Amazon (www.amazon.com)

Amazon is the internet's retailing success story. Though it has had its ups and downs like most 'dinosaurs' of eCommerce – Amazon first started operations in 1995 – today it is a thriving retail business in its own right, and also provides a third party marketplace for you to gain access to its considerable customer base. It operates local sites in the US, Canada, the UK, Germany, Italy and Japan, among others. Amazon originally began as a media retailer, starting with books and soon expanding into music and movies. Before long, it launched ranges in electronics and fashion, and today has a breadth of products that rivals eBay's.

Why Consider Using Amazon?

- Amazon's various global websites attract more than 2.3 million Australian visitors each month. It is an internet rarity: a site that has managed to attract an enormous share of Australian spend without having an Australian website, local warehouse or active marketing campaigns targeting Australian consumers generally.
- Its US website attracts more than 65 million visitors each month, according to Wikipedia.
- At the time of writing, there was strong industry speculation that Amazon would soon be opening an Australian warehouse as a base to distribute Australian retailers' products globally. Australians will continue shopping on their favourite Amazon site, but an

increasing number of Australian products will be visible to them and, if purchased, these products will be distributed by Amazon's highly efficient logistics operations from within Australia.

- Unlike a lot of other marketplaces, Amazon offers some of its customers outside Australia this highly competitive logistics service. It will handle all aspects of the sale – from displaying the product to customers, accepting payment, packing and posting, and handling any returns or complaints as well. (In a move to offer similar services in the US, eBay recently acquired a company called GSI Commerce (www.gsicommerce.com), which currently handles fulfilment for some of the US's largest retailers.) Like those options outlined in Chapter One, however, by outsourcing sales management to a third party, you are losing ownership of the customer and this cannot be the best option for your business longer term. Alternatively, like eBay, you can simply use the site for exposure and handle all the order fulfilment yourself.

- Amazon has one of the world's most efficient search engines, which highlights complementary and relevant products to its customers with great efficiency. It has the ability to remember buyers' search sessions and previous purchases to make recommendations tailored specifically to each buyer. While a lot of websites have this ability, Amazon's is arguably the world's best. For your business, this means that buyers interested in your products should be able to find them more easily on this site than other marketplaces.

- Amazon's mobile app (available at the iTunes store) means your products will be available via mobile and can be purchased anytime, anywhere, without you having to invest in mobile development. Other mobile apps can be found by searching 'mobile' within Amazon's Help pages.

- Be conscious of the fact that Amazon is also the largest retailer in its own marketplace. This means that, effectively, you are competing with the marketplace owner and it generally has the ability to source and sell your products at a much more competitive rate than you, and to use data to know which products it should prioritise within its own inventory.

- Amazon's fees to sell are commensurate with the experience it offers its buyers. At the time of writing, its published fee rates on the US site, for example, ranged from 6 to 25 per cent per item sold plus a fixed 99 cent 'closing fee'.

How to Use Amazon – Top Tips

1. If listing in high volumes, subscribe to become a Pro Merchant seller – fees are cheaper and the fixed closing fee is waived.
2. Before you begin, view the useful Amazon Video Workshops, which can be found on Amazon's Help pages. Topics include your seller account, product

details page, listings process, getting paid and managing orders.

3. Webstore by Amazon gives you the ability to launch your stand-alone website as well as listing on the Amazon marketplace, but you need to be a Pro Merchant subscriber.

4. Consider using its Fulfilment by Amazon (FBA) service if you are trying to expand your business to a global audience – Amazon will store your products and distribute them to your buyers. FBA products receive additional exposure on Amazon's pages and buyers gain access to additional Amazon services like gift wrapping and one-day delivery.

5. Aim for Featured Merchant status to help your products stand out from your competitors'. Featured Merchants are Pro Merchant subscribers who meet a minimum service standard and other performance-based criteria.

6. Get more support and up-to-the-minute tips from Amazon's seller support blog located at www.amazonsellersupportblog.com.

Gumtree (www.gumtree.com.au)

Gumtree only accepts individual listings (or ads) and has no provision for mass uploading so it is difficult to apply a scalable strategy to the site but it is free traffic so it's worth considering. Unlike the other marketplaces mentioned above, Gumtree is particularly strong in non-hard-goods categories like services, jobs, accommodation and also in vehicles. If any of these categories are applicable for your business, then this is a site you should definitely consider. Gumtree has boomed in the past 18 months, with strong word of mouth and a high rotation television advertisement driving a considerable increase in site traffic. Owned by eBay, Gumtree is effectively a free classifieds site, a place where your business can advertise in selected categories, but where no transactions take place online.

Why Consider Using Gumtree?

- More than 1.5 million Australians visit the site each month.
- It is free to advertise on the site, with no sale (or transaction) fee attached.
- It offers a truly local experience where people in your area can find your business and come to shop with you face to face.
- It's a simple-to-use site with a basic listing process that takes only a minute or two to complete but there are no provisions for bulk upload of advertisements.

How to Use Gumtree – Top Tips

1. Start by choosing your local city/area and displaying your ads to your local buyer base.

2. Be clear and concise in your advertisement – Gumtree users are not used to extensive text and are looking for a fast and convenient process.

3. As you are restricted in the number of advertisements you can upload, choose your 'hero' product or service – that is your most popular one at the best price – and use it to entice more buyers.

4. Clearly outline your contact details and be prepared to answer phone calls and emails immediately.

Trading Post (www.tradingpost.com.au)

Trading Post is somewhat of an iconic Australian brand. It has been in operation since 1966 and was among the earliest and most successful 'trading' brands in this country. Beginning as a print publication, the business moved online early but in recent years has struggled to maintain momentum. Purchased by Telstra for a reported $636 million, in 2008 it closed down its print operations and became an online-only business and today it attracts a relatively modest number of Australians each month. At the time of writing its traffic figures were down 7 per cent compared to the previous year. Nevertheless, Trading Post is a brand that Australians know and love, and its free listing for items under $500 makes it an option well worth considering for your business.

Why Consider Using Trading Post?

- Around 600 000 Australians still visit the site each month.
- There are no upfront listing fees for items under $500; it costs $19.95 to advertise items above $500, other than vehicles.
- It is particularly strong in the vehicles category.
- Unlike most other marketplaces, you can use American Express and Diner's Club credit cards to pay your selling fees.
- It accepts payment mechanisms such as PayPal and Paymate.

How to Use Trading Post – Top Tips

1. To upload multiple ads, download Trading Post's template file from the site and use Excel to create your inventory list.
2. Ensure you provide clear business information for your ad – it is required by law in some states – and check the box 'mark as business' when you upload your ad.
3. Share your ads via social media sites like Facebook and Twitter (see Chapter Seven) by clicking on the relevant icons next to the image(s) that you upload or the links in the Ad Confirmation you receive once it is uploaded.
4. Consider paying for optional features that will help your ads stand out from other listings.
5. It's easy to upload videos to your Trading Post ads, but make sure they are informative and entertaining. Once

you upload your ad, you will receive an option to add a video on the confirmation page.

6. Business ads also have their logo appear in search results – make sure your logo is clear and readable for the size that Trading Post allows.

Who's doing it well?

- Renovation Boys (www.renovationboys. com.au) use Trading Post well to list a wide selection of their bathroom range and sponsor the Home/Renovation category on the site.
- Trading Post has 74 pages of used-car dealers who bulk upload cars to the site.
- A complete list of dealers and sellers can be found at www.tradingpost.com.au/Dealer.

Quick Sales (www.quicksales.com.au)

Quick Sales began as Oztion (pronounced *oz-shun*), an Aussie alternative to eBay, and it provided a local auction-driven platform at cheaper rates than eBay. Purchased by the carsales group in 2010 for a reported $1.1 million, they immediately changed its name to Quick Sales, as Oztion struggled to get brand recognition and consumers generally had trouble pronouncing it properly. In addition, as the popularity of auctions as a buying format decreased, it was dangerous to brand the entire business with that format. Today it remains unclear how much of an investment the carsales group intends to make in the site and it generally has low consumer awareness – what drives most of its traffic is a group of sellers whose disgruntlement with other marketplaces is balanced by a trade-off in reduced fees.

Why Consider Using Quick Sales?

- 450 000 Australians visit the site each month and there are 550 000 members.
- Sale fees that start as low as 4.5 per cent for items sold, and most listings have no upfront fees.
- Like eBay, Quick Sales have stores (or vShops) that allow you to have all your products in one convenient location for buyers. They start at $5 per month.
- With backing by the significantly sized (and highly profitable) carsales group, the site could be the subject of a marketing campaign at some point in the future and, if it drives enough traffic, early adopters of the site will benefit.
- At the time of writing, there were just over 500 000 items for sale on the site, arguably making it easier for buyers to find your items in this marketplace compared to others that have millions of items for sale at any time.
- Its listings are live on the site for 60 days, or until sold.

How to Use Quick Sales – Top Tips

1. The site offers Australia Post verification (Australia Post staff members confirm your identity after you show them documentation). Using this feature should help to increase buyer confidence.

2. Unlike eBay, you can use a paid advertising feature called Ad-tion, which shows your listings on key pages on the site and the minimum spend starts at just $10 for 30 days.

3. vShops allow you to customise and brand your Quick Sales presence and have the added feature of a cart that allows buyers to purchase from multiple stores but only go to the checkout once.

4. Use the site's Express Lister to bulk upload your inventory via a Windows-based program.

5. Feature a link to Quick Sales from your own website to earn referral credits to reduce the fees you pay for using the site by between $2 and $4 per referral.

Who's doing it well?

- Small businesses without their own website are generally the most active on Quick Sales. Its lower fees and no upfront costs make it a risk-free alternative to eBay, though buyer numbers are significantly lower.
- Balance the time and effort required to upload and maintain your listings versus the expected return from a small buyer base.

Alibaba (www.alibaba.com)

Though you may not have heard of it, Alibaba is a hugely successful third party business-to-business marketplace operating out of Asia. Launched in 1998, today the business's first half 2011 profit was reported at over US$140 million. The site operates in both English and Chinese. Australians also have the option of going direct to a special sub-site located at au.alibaba.com.

Why Consider Using Alibaba?

- Buyers have increased confidence on the site as payments are made via escrow, that is, the funds are not released to the seller until the buyer has received the goods and confirmed they are happy with them.

- It attracts customers from 240 countries and regions with around 70 million registered users, 21 million of whom are on its international marketplaces; the remainder are in China.
- Over 500 000 Australians visit the site each month – generally they are businesses looking for opportunities to buy products in bulk and re-sell locally.
- At the end of the 2011 financial year, traffic to international marketplaces had grown a phenomenal 65 per cent compared to the previous year, signifying the heightened popularity of the site with non-Chinese users.
- It's one of the most active business-to-business websites in the world and a cost-effective way to get your products sold in bulk globally.

How to Use Alibaba – Top Tips

1. Take advantage of the site's offer of displaying up to 50 products for free.
2. Become a Gold Supplier (the site claims that Gold Suppliers get up to 22 times more enquiries than other suppliers) to receive premium exposure on the site.
3. Utilise the site's Keyword Ranking system, which allows you to purchase keywords for premium placement in search results.
4. Use multiple accounts to provide more options for buyers – consider discounting products in one account but maintaining higher prices in another so that your

buyers have a choice of a premium offering without you losing overall sales.

5. If you are looking for more B2C (business to consumer, or direct to consumer) opportunities, consider using Alibaba's sister site, Taobao (www.taobao.com) – China's largest consumer trading platform. If you have products that are unique to the Chinese market, you may find a niche.

Who's doing it well?

- You can find a list of Australian companies selling on the site by clicking the Suppliers tab at the top of the page, use the 'Select Country/ Region' drop-down list to choose Australia, and enter a keyword for your category before clicking 'Search'.

Westfield (www.westfield.com.au)

Synonymous with retail, Westfield is listed on the Australian stock exchange and manages more than a hundred shopping centres around the world with a combined mass of more than 25 000 retailers. The company has total assets of around $59 billion. It launched its online mall in late 2010.

Why Consider Using Westfield?

- Around 400 000 Australians visit the site each month.
- It's the marketplace that has attracted the most Australian retailers – display your products alongside some of the most recognised retail brands in Australia.
- It's the only Australian marketplace that offers a 'premium' experience, where most products are sold at full retail price.
- Note that Westfield charges you upfront rent to appear on the site and, depending on the size of your business, will charge between 10 and 25 per cent of the sale price. (Though Westfield do not advertise their fees on the site, this is what most businesses should expect.)

Who's doing it well?

- Westfield is home to popular retail brands including Bardot, Ben Sherman, ECCO, GUESS, JB Hi-Fi, Katies, Oxford and SABA.
- Westfield also accepts products from online-only e-tailers including Cellarmasters, iSubscribe and Roses Only.

How to Use Westfield

Strangely, Westfield does not display information on how best to access its marketplace and prefers to conduct one-on-one negotiations and agreements with businesses. Contact the site for more information on how you can display your products.

Trade Me (www.trademe.co.nz)

Founded in 1999 and purchased by the Fairfax Digital group in 2006 for a reported NZ$700 million, Trade Me is New Zealand's answer to eBay. It has a monopoly on the New Zealand market and is the leader in most of the categories in which it operates, including goods for sale, services, jobs, real estate and vehicles.

Why Consider Using Trade Me?

- It's a cost-effective and fast solution to expanding into the New Zealand market without having to open a local office or warehouse or investing in local operations.
- Over 100 000 Australians visit the site each month.
- Trade Me has around 2.4 million active members according to Wikipedia – the whole country only has around 4 million people!
- It has competitive fee rates with the sale fee starting at 7.5 per cent per item sold; most products have no upfront fees to list.

- Trade Me more or less has a monopoly in the New Zealand market (eBay has a very small presence, for example) so if you are considering expanding into New Zealand, it really is the only marketplace option worth considering.

How to Use Trade Me – Top Tips

1. You will need to open a New Zealand bank account in order to use the site.
2. Conduct thorough research on the best and cheapest methods to send your products to New Zealand (refer to Chapter Five) as you will be competing with domestic sellers who arguably have lower postage costs.
3. Accept payments in New Zealand dollars and don't try to force buyers into using Australian dollars.
4. If your business is large enough, and you offer telephone customer support, consider paying for a local New Zealand number that diverts to your Australian business.
5. Join Trade Me's Retail Programme for account management, bulk upload support and other insights. Details are on the website.

Other Category Sites

Depending on the category your business operates in, you are more than likely going to find a marketplace that allows you to advertise your goods or services. Some of these sites restrict the number of ads or listings available for business sellers, others have no restrictions. The vast majority come with some sort of fee – whether that be upfront fees (pay to appear on the site whether you successfully sell the good or service, or not), sale fee (usually a percentage fee payable only when a buyer enters into a transaction with you), click-through fee (payable only when a customer clicks on your listing), subscription fees (usually monthly access fees), or a combination of some or all of them.

Below is a list of some of the more common category-specific sites. An internet search will reveal a host of other options relevant to your business.

- Cars & other vehicles: Car Sales (www.carsales.com.au), Trading Post (refer above), Gumtree (refer above), Drive (www.drive.com.au), Cars Guide (www.carsguide.com.au)
- Accommodation: Stayz (www.stayz.com.au), Take a Break (www.takeabreak.com.au), Bookastay (www.holidayrentals.com.au)
- Travel: Expedia (www.expedia.com.au), Last Minute (www.lastminute.com.au), Wotif (www.wotif.com.au), Hotels.Com (www.hotels.com)
- Real Estate: Real Estate (www.realestate.com.au), Domain (www.domain.com.au), Homehound (www.homehound.com.au)
- Restaurants & bars: Eatability (www.eatability.com.au), Restaurants.com.au (www.restaurants.com.au), Restaurant Guide (www.restaurant.org.au), Mietta's (www.miettas.com)

- Services & trades: Trade Connect (www.tradeconnect.
  com.au), Service Central (www.servicecentral.com.au)
- Arts & crafts: Etsy (www.etsy.com), Markets Online
  (www.marketsonline.com.au), Art Gallery Australia
  (www.artgalleryaustralia.com.au), The Art Box (www.
  theartbox.com.au)
- General Directories: Yellow Pages (www.yellowpages.
  com.au), White Pages (www.whitepages.com.au),
  TrueLocal (www.truelocal.com.au), Pink Pages (www.
  pinkpages.com.au)
- Careers: MyCareer (www.mycareer.com.au), SEEK
  (www.seek.com.au), Career One (www.careerone.com.
  au), Jobs (www.jobs.com.au)

Homework:

List five items or services on your preferred marketplace and make note of how long it took to list, how many people viewed your items, how many sold, and what the total cost of sale was. This will be useful later in Chapter Ten when we create a prioritised action plan for getting your business online.

CHAPTER SUMMARY

- You understand what online marketplaces are, and whether they are applicable for your business.

- You know how to evaluate which marketplace/s is/are the best options for your business and you have prioritised which one/s you will begin displaying your business on.

- You have registered as a seller on your prioritised site, and begun using the site as a buyer to better understand how it operates, and the price of goods/services and level of service offered by competing sellers.

- You have conducted thorough research on the site to make a shortlist of products/services you intend to list on the site.

- You have investigated the various options available to you for streamlining the listing process, inventory management process and post-sales process.

Interview with Deborah Sharkey
Vice President and Managing Director
eBay Australia and New Zealand Pty Ltd

What are some of the common misperceptions about eCommerce?

The importance of an online strategy is still misunderstood. The internet now forms an integral part of our everyday lives – changing the way we communicate, stay informed, get entertainment and shop. With over 10 million Australians now shopping online, eCommerce has hit a critical inflection point in the local retail sector. It is the biggest catalyst for growth in the retail industry today, creating significant opportunity for manufacturers, retailers and logistics providers who are prepared to evolve and meet the needs of the modern consumer.

What is your best advice for small and medium-sized businesses wanting to sell online but not knowing where to start?

Many small to medium-sized Australian retail businesses are recognising the value of online as an essential part of their multi-channel sales strategy. This simply means being everywhere that your customer is. Today six million Australians visit eBay every month; that's 60 per cent of Australia's online shopping population, making eBay the nation's most popular online shopping site. Thus, eBay is a powerful option for all businesses looking for the most cost-effective path to the online consumer.

Why do you think the larger retailers in Australia have been slow to embrace online?

There are lots of theories around that but we are delighted that an increasing number of brands and retailers are heading in the right direction. A number of Australia's most recognisable and sought-after brands, such as Witchery, Alannah Hill, Mimco, Supré and Seafolly have recently launched on eBay's new fashion destination – the Fashion Gallery, offering consumers a selection of brand-new products and sale items at a significant discount to retail, all at a fixed price. With online fashion sales expected to reach $3.4 billion by 2015, many brands are now recognising Australia's growing appetite to browse and buy a broad range of fashion items online.

How big is the online opportunity? Today it's only about 5 per cent of retail; how much scope does it have for growth?

There is still tremendous eCommerce growth yet to come in Australia. The buoyant eCommerce growth is in striking contrast to overall retail, which has been flat for over a year now (0.1 per cent in March 2011). We have seen this growth on eBay, where the largest 2000 Australian businesses selling on eBay grew a phenomenal 38 per cent last year. Australian shoppers are spending, on average, 1 hour and 40 minutes shopping online each week, purchasing travel, groceries, fashion, electronics and computers. They spent $27 billion online in 2010, and that amount was forecast to increase by 12 per cent in 2011.

How does eBay help facilitate success for online businesses?

With over six million Australian visitors a month, eBay is the most cost-effective online marketing channel there is. eBay invests in traffic generation, mobile innovation and other leading-edge online technologies so its merchants don't have to. We also know that in order to nurture further growth, it is critical that we continue to work to build logistics infrastructure in Australia and we are partnering with Australia Post and other shipping providers for the benefit of businesses on eBay.

3

Designing a Successful Website

Designing a website your customers will love

WHAT THIS CHAPTER WILL COVER

- Why having your own website is critical for your eCommerce success

- Who should design and write your website

- The importance of photography and video

- A guide to how much your website should cost to create

- The importance of keeping your website up to date

- Website essentials – five things your website must have

- Buyer expectations – five website features your buyers demand

---

Do I Need a Website?

In the previous two chapters we learnt that there are options for getting your business online without having to create your own website. While some of these options are very effective at quickly selling products or services, some are highly cost-effective and some allow you to retain your branding, very few of them let you own the customer. Having your own website allows you to:

- Get to know more about your customers, understand their shopping habits better and what they like and dislike about your business.
- Contact buyers when you wish to offer them other relevant products from your range, discounts, specials and any other form of marketing communication to help drive your business.
- Control the entire customer experience from beginning to end.
- Design your own search functionality and not be at the whim of an algorithm on another site that is not only difficult to understand, but also constantly changing.
- Control your own buying flow and merchandising, so you can choose to display whichever products you like, to whichever customers you like, in whatever part of your website.
- Design your own website and form, unrestricted by the boundaries of an existing website.
- Have your choice of checkout options and payment methods.

- Most importantly of all ... have your own rules and your terms of trade. As long as you don't break the law, you won't have to get to know the thousands of third-party rules, read long user agreements and extensive policies, and be in constant fear of breaking any of them.

As I mentioned in the introduction to this book, *not* having a website is not an option for your business. Even if you do not currently sell directly to the public – that is, you are a designer or a manufacturer – having a website means that you will be able to control the presentation and branding of your products. Don't allow re-sellers to control your image unless you have one who will do the best possible job of promoting your products for you. More information about channel conflict is covered later in this chapter.

Who can Design my Website?

There are literally thousands of options available to your business. An entire web design industry now exists and an internet search will show you page after page of service providers who can design a website for you right now. You can choose between having the website designed for you locally or overseas, by an agency or independent designer who will create a bespoke design (one tailored to your specifications). You provide the site designer with a brief and work closely with them on a design that best reflects what is in your mind. A lot of them will also be able to do this for you remotely, communicating with you online or over the phone, so you may never need to go to their place of business. Research thoroughly and ask to see a list of clients so you can decide if you like the design abilities of the agency. Most importantly, see if you can speak to one or two of their clients to ask if they are happy with the performance of the website, and the service delivered by the agency.

There are also off-the-shelf options. Go into a software store and buy a package that allows you to design a website yourself, or else conduct an internet search and find downloadable templates or tools that can help you do this.

In a helpful comparison of software packages, www. toptenreviews.com suggested that Web Easy Professional, Intuit, Web Studio, Yola Silver and Xara were the top five solutions to consider. Some of these are available in Australia so check online or with your local software retailer.

A further option is to use a different kind of agency – one that can build you a website solution that includes the design and function of your website, but also includes backend solutions such as inventory management systems and the ability to have your products appear on your own website as well as marketplaces (like the ones outlined in Chapter Two), while others will also manage the complete process for you, including logistics, warehousing and customer service. See below for more information.

Website Management – Third Parties and Products

There is a range of agencies and ready-made products that can manage the building and inventory integration of your website. Each agency offers a different type of service and a different cost, and has a pre-built solution that can link in with your current inventory system and upload your products to some marketplaces. You should consider which marketplaces you wish to use and whether the solution has the ability to upload to it. Before choosing an agency, ask for a list of their existing clients and visit those clients' websites to see if you like their functionality and design. Also conduct an internet search for the client and the products they sell to see how high they appear on the search results list – there is no point having a beautiful website that no one can find.

Here are some of the products you should consider for your business but a word of warning: avoid being locked into long-term contracts and be mindful of the fact that you may, under some agreements, be relinquishing the ability to manage your website yourself and therefore updating it can be an expensive and time-consuming process.

1. **Magento** (www.magentocommerce.com) is a global solution recently purchased by eBay. Offers businesses control over the functionality and design of their website, order management, search engine optimisation, marketing tools, and multiple shipping and payment options. Clients include Nokia, Breville,

Bing Lee, Ford and Goodyear. Connects with eBay and Google Shopping.

2. **Powerfront** (www.powerfront.com) provides a complete web solution including website design, eCommerce functionality, content management system, search engine optimisation, website hosting and customer communications. Clients include Toys "R" Us, House, Oroton, LG, Sportscraft and Ted's Cameras.

3. **eCorner** (www.ecorner.com.au) has its registered ePages software, which includes a cloud-based solution for eCommerce, message security and web analytics. Clients include Dick Smith, Getprice and Urban Baby.

4. **Channel Advisor** (www.channeladvisor.com) takes your product inventory and uploads to various online channels. Webstores allow for customisable design of your site. Clients include GolfEtail, Voodoo and a host of eBay sellers. Connects with eBay, Google Shopping, Bing, Amazon and Shopping.com.

5. **Neto** (www.neto.com.au) offers an all-in-one hosted shopping cart and website design that integrates with a variety of accounting, freight and marketing channels and payment systems. Clients include Hoselink. Connects with eBay, Shopping.com and Getprice.

An internet search will reveal a host of other options so conduct your research thoroughly and speak to a variety of providers before deciding which solution will work best for your business.

Who Should Write my Website Content?

While you know your business and its products or service better than anyone, writing online copy (or content) is a specialised skill. The way people read online is different from how they read physical items and there is an art to balancing how thorough online content should be with how easy it is to read. Remember, you are trying to convey everything about your products and business; potentially to someone who has never had anything to do with you before. The tone of the content is just as important in conveying your business's brand as the logo or even your business name. While it is unlikely that creating the content yourself will damage your business, online copywriters may help enhance your sales and online reputation beyond your creative abilities.

One very important note to make: do everything in your power to ensure you have no spelling errors. Triple-check every word yourself and ask friends and family to read content very carefully. Repeatedly misspelling words creates the overall impression that your business is unprofessional.

Finally, all creativity and accuracy aside, a well-written website will actually drive more traffic and, more importantly, it will be better quality traffic, that is, buyers specifically looking for your products or business. Search engine optimisation (SEO) is the science of writing a website in a manner that allows search engine bots from Google, Bing, Yahoo! and the like to accurately read your content and automatically show your website in search result lists when buyers are searching for your business, products or services. More of this is covered in Chapter Six.

How Important are Photography and Video?

Aside from price, pictures can often help buyers decide whether to purchase your items. Your website should emulate the highest quality catalogue or brochure in the offline world. Photographs of your items need to be professionally executed. Here are some basic tips:

- Use natural lighting wherever possible. If using artificial light, professional photographers can give expert advice on the best equipment to use.
- Use a plain, preferably white, background. Let the products be the hero.
- Do not use a zoom; bring the camera closer to the product.
- Take photographs from a number of angles and upload these to your website, don't just provide a front-on view of the product.
- For textures and finer patterns, take close-up images. Consider using a magnifying functionality on your site to help buyers see these details as clearly as possible.

- When you upload your images, label them concisely; this will help in your search engine optimisation (refer to Chapter Six).
- Always clearly label the dimensions of the product.
- Protect your intellectual property by watermarking your images, or adding copyright symbols. If you use a professional photographer, make sure you retain ownership of the images and are aware of whether you need to give credits to the photographer on your website.
- If you sell services that result in a physical outcome (renovations, art work, carpentry, etc.), show photographs from your portfolio.
- Three-dimensional imaging products are expensive but add an outstanding quality to your website and showcase your products better than any form of two-dimensional photography.

Today, effective use of video can be an additional, low-cost method of marketing your products and/or services to a wider audience. Consider using video on your website, particularly if your product is complicated to use, or would benefit from a physical demonstration. If your products or services have been featured in advertisements or reviewed on television, these clips can also be helpful on your site (ensure you have permission to use these). Keep your clips short – less than three minutes where possible – and aim for content that is punchy, informative and entertaining. No one has the time to watch a boring or unprofessional video, and this will just result in turning your customers away. Always remember your target customer and tailor your content to them specifically – while you might think it's cute to have your child star in an online infomercial, if your target audience are teenagers, they are unlikely to connect.

Getting Straight Down to Business – Keep an Uncomplicated Website

I recently went looking for a gift for a friend who'd just had a baby. There was a particular product I had in mind but after briefly searching eBay and Google, I had trouble finding an Australian business that sold it. Instead, I went to the manufacturer's foreign website and, though it was beautifully designed, it featured animation that was not only slow to load and could not be skipped, it distracted me from their products and the information I wanted to see: price, details and whether there was a recommended Australian retailer. I immediately left the website and went back to Google to trawl through page after page of results until I found an Australian e-tailer that stocked the product.

An eCommerce website needs to be just about that: commerce. Don't be tempted to distract your buyers with content that looks pretty but only serves to delay the buyer from transacting. Online shopping attention spans can be very limited as the majority of shoppers are driven by price *and* convenience. When speaking to your web designer, make sure you give clear directions that the site should be fast and free from complicated programs or scripts. Your products or services should always be the focus of the website, and getting to a product page should be no more than one or two clicks away from your homepage – avoid anything that may take time to load before the buyer can move on. Your servers at work might be much faster than the average buyer's at home and what takes seconds for you to see might take minutes for your buyer to download.

Once your buyers are on a product page (that is, the page outlining what is for sale with a clear picture and price), do not distract them with anything. The action-oriented link to purchase or add to a shopping cart should be the main thing buyers see, and the next logical course of action. Always utilise shopping cart functionality to ensure your buyers are enticed to buy more, and can use the checkout for all items at once rather than having to pay for them individually, or waiting for you to manually combine them into one invoice.

How Much Should my Website Cost to Build?

It is difficult to give any business an exact guide on what is reasonable, and what is not. A perfectly functional website might cost you as little as $2000–$5000 but it all depends on how complicated the site needs to be, how many products it needs to display (or how many pages the site needs to include) and whether your site requires specific skills or software to build, all of which cost extra money. It's certainly not unheard of for medium-sized businesses to spend $10 000–$50 000 on a website, and larger businesses to spend over $500 000.

Create a business plan that forecasts the volume of sales you expect to do online over the next three, five and ten years. The cost of creating your website should be commensurate with that, and a rough parameter would be your cost of physical rent. If you pay your landlord 15 per cent of your annual turnover in rent, and forecast your internet sales to be $100 000 per year over the next three years, then you wouldn't normally want to spend more than $45 000 on creating your website in total (marketing and other costs of running an online business like customer service, etc., are additional). On the other hand, some online templates are free to use and for a small business or service provider this could prove entirely adequate.

It is possible to download the website templates for free but they are generally inflexible and will restrict how you can present your products and business to your customers. Depending on the scale of your operations, though, they may provide a good entry point into online. These can be found by conducting an internet search and one worth checking out is Google's template – it promises to get you online in less than 15 minutes! Details can be found at www. gettingbusinessonline.com.au, for one year's free website hosting, a free domain name for two years and $75 worth of free Google advertising.

How Often Should I Update my Website?

It depends on how cutting edge your original website design is but as a guide, you should certainly consider updating your website's look, feel and functionality at least every 18 months. Be careful not to radically overhaul your website if it is attracting a significant number of users each month because there are countless internet stories of businesses that overhauled their websites, thinking they were doing the right thing by their customers, only to experience mass revolt and diminished trade as a result. But you should certainly consider your website as a living part of your business, one that will need regular attention. Just as you would change around the design and layout of your store, or move products from one area to another, change your shop window and the like, so your website needs to remain fresh. No other industry changes as quickly as online. Ten years ago, for example, very few websites accepted PayPal as a payment mechanism, and Facebook and Twitter links did not exist – now they are critical components of most online businesses.

Website Business Essentials – Five Things your Website Must Have

1. *Your Website Should List your Entire Inventory*

Here's why. Let's say you are a national retailer with 40 stores. Your average customer has been a loyal shopper at your chain of stores for the past 15 years, and in that time, they have visited at least eight of them. The customer has built up an impression of the types of products you sell, the range of products and the price you offer them at. This is why they continue to buy from you. Having never shopped online with you before, one day your buyer learns that you have launched a new website. Deciding to try it out, they type in your URL and what do they find? The branding and look and feel of the website is familiar and reassuring, so they go to their favourite category – books – to browse what is available online. Just two weeks ago they were in one of your stores deciding which of three cookbooks to buy and now they have decided on two of them. They browse the cookbook section of your website and, after looking for 15 minutes, cannot find any of the three they had in mind. Deciding on a different strategy, they type in each of the three book titles but again waste five minutes because they are unable to find any of them on your website.

What do you think happens next? More than likely, the buyer leaves your website and looks for those books elsewhere. If you are lucky, they will come back into one of your stores to purchase them but what will probably happen – as they want to begin their online shopping – is they will choose to purchase the books from another website. This experience has further implications for the buyer, as next time they want any books, their lasting impression is that your business will not have what they want in stock. They may choose not to visit any of your stores for books again and while you might have your complete range of toys available online, they don't think to come back to your site to check for any other products because their perception is that the website has a poorer selection than the physical store. Then, they probably tell their friends that the online experience is not as good as the store . . . and you lose not only this customer for online transactions, but their friends as well. Even if you expand your range at a later date to include the same books as you generally offer in store, it's unlikely you'll be able to lure this customer back in the future.

As more Australians choose to shop online, their expectation is that their online experience will closely mirror the experience you can provide them in person. Unless your product or service cannot be purchased from any website anywhere else in the world, savvy buyers will undoubtedly source it from elsewhere and you will be losing not only an online customer, but the offline one as well. As mentioned previously, this includes utilising shopping cart facilities so your buyers can pay for multiple purchases in one transaction.

Who's doing it well?

- JB Hi-Fi (www.jbhifi.com.au) has a very broad range of products available online, closely mirroring what is available in the average store.

2. *Your Website Should be Transactional*

It is for the reason outlined above that you must have a website which people can use to purchase online, not just for research. Buyers will likely find it *more* frustrating to find a product on your website but be unable to purchase it online, than they will not being able to find the product at all. Similar to the example above, unless someone is online for the sole purpose of researching products and having no intention of buying immediately would they be satisfied with a website that is not transactional?

If you do not sell direct to the public yourself, always provide a list of both online sellers (link directly to each) and offline places where your products or service can be purchased. Be sure to provide the links from each product page, and link directly to the individual product for sale on the re-seller site, rather than providing a generic list of places to buy and redirecting traffic to a homepage that then requires the buyer to start their product search all over again.

A note about channel conflict: If you are the manufacturer of a product, should you sell direct to the public online? This is a question more Australian manufacturers are asking themselves and, increasingly, answering with a resounding yes. Unless your retailers are stocking your complete range, buying reasonable quantities of all your products at a solid margin, selling these products via their online store and helping to preserve the strong reputation of your business overall, why should you limit the growth of your business by refusing to sell direct to consumers online? Some manufacturers have discovered that they can sell direct to consumers at significantly less than retail price, but still make more margin for themselves and, at the same time, retain ownership of the customer to help build brand loyalty. As Australian retailers fail to embrace online, your customers are probably turning to international sellers of your type of products. The decision to sell direct is one that will carefully need to balance the size of the overall retail market with the anticipated size of the online opportunity and the relationship you currently have with your retailers.

3. *Your Online Prices Should Never be Higher than your Offline Ones – Aim to Make Online Cheaper*

Because the internet is effectively the world's largest and most effective price comparison engine, you need to ensure you remain competitive on price. Buyers who are conscious of your offline pricing and learn that your web prices are more expensive will stop visiting your website immediately, possibly never to return. If it is discounted offline, it must also be discounted online. Most buyers see the internet as a place to source bargains or save money. A report by The Australia Institute showed that 85 per cent of respondents went online in an attempt to save money.[5] Buyers are also savvy to the fact that online businesses generally have lower overheads than offline ones – lower rents, fewer staff, lower marketing costs – and rightly or wrongly, as a result, they generally expect these savings to be passed on to them. It is often expected, therefore, that online prices will be lower than offline ones.

As a general rule, price your items consistently between online and offline channels. Unless you have unique products or a unique offering – service, interest-free finance, free postage, to name but a few – don't expect to have a significant share of the online market unless you are price competitive.

4. *Your Website Should Store the Contact and Payment Details of your Customers*

Don't make people register their details just to browse your site. Generally they won't and will choose not to return. If you do want people to become registered members once they purchase, only do so as part of the checkout flow. Make log in as easy as possible for buyers, but secure enough to protect them from hacking. Like price, buyers are also driven by convenience so if they are a repeat customer, they will not want to enter in their payment or address details every time. Ensure you comply with all relevant laws if you do create a website that stores your customers' personal or financial information, and ensure you have a dedicated page on your site reassuring buyers how their personal information is kept securely.

> ## Who's doing it well?
>
> - Amazon is a stand-out performer in this category. If you have not purchased from them before, it is a seamless checkout process. Once signed in, I never have to re-enter credit card information and I can choose from a list of all previous addresses to which I've had items sent (for example, home, work, presents sent to family members).

5. *Make your Website Data Configured*

Data, and understanding it, is at the core of any online business's success. What do I mean by that? If you build a website today, it is practically impossible to predict just how many people will be visiting it, or buying from it, in years to come. You need to plan for a future where online could be the entirety of your business and then ask yourself what you need to know about your customers, and how they use your site.

> Competitive intelligence can help you grow your online business based on facts, not guess work. Using Terapeak provides you with direct insight into product pricing, supply and demand, and market trends. Market intelligence is absolutely a key factor in any online merchant's success.
>
> *Anthony Sukow, Executive Vice President and Co-Founder, Terapeak*

Data can tell you the following things:

- Where visitors were before your site, such as referring domains like Google, or another site you have placed an advertisement on.
- How they found your site – which keywords they entered.
- Where they clicked – what parts of your site are performing well, and which could be optimised with better content. Where most people are clicking is prime real estate and should therefore be where you place your most important content.
- The IP address of your visitors, which allows you to track where your customers are from, but also recognise each of them individually and therefore serve them content that is relevant to their needs and desires.

- What your buyers are searching for as well as buying – is there a discrepancy between the two, and how can you turn more searches into purchases?
- Automatically identify repeat customers and your most loyal customers to offer them discounts and other special offers.
- Identify which customers are opening which emails you send, and what they click on within each email.
- At what point do customers leave your site – and is there anything you can do to encourage them to stay longer and purchase more?

This just scratches the surface of the importance of data in running an online business. Not only will you be able to know more about your business, and optimise it accordingly, but other businesses may wish to leverage your customer base in joint or cross-promotion and this can become a revenue-raising stream in its own right (subject to your user agreement and privacy laws, of course).

Alexa (www.alexa.com) is a great source of free information for website traffic and tools offered by Google Analytics (www.google.com.au/analytics/), Experian Hitwise (www.experian.com.au/hitwise/) and Adobe Digital Marketing Suite (www.omniture.com) will help you understand more about how your customers are finding you. Quantium's WebScout program (www.quantium.com. au) can help you better understand your competitors, their range of supply online and the prices they offer.

Meeting Buyer Expectations: Five Website Features your Buyers Demand (and an Extra One They'll Love)

1. *Search Functionality and Taxonomy*

First and foremost, once they get to your website, buyers want to be able to find your products or services easily. Place your search field prominently at the top of the page with a clear call to action – that is, a button next to the field saying 'search', 'find it' or similar. There is a very good reason that Google's homepage defaults to a search field on a white background, it encourages users to do only one thing: search what they are looking for. Talk to your website designer about how best to configure your search: will buyers be able to find all the content on your site or just the products; will the search look in both product title and description; will you automatically include synonyms (so that when a buyer types in hat, you also show all caps, for example)? Your search functionality only needs to be as complicated as your range is diverse.

If you don't have search functionality you will more than likely have a category tree helping buyers browse for items. On eBay, for example, there are tens of thousands of product categories. The advice here is to think like a physical store. How do stores who stock items similar to what you are selling organise their products? Most category trees have quite broad parents, or branches, that then break down over one or more levels into leaves. If I use dresses as an example, you might typically see a category structure that looks like this:

Clothing > Women's Clothing > Dresses >
Dress Styles > Sizes

Be careful not to make your category taxonomy too complex. Not only will it make it more difficult for buyers to find
what they are looking for and complicate your site with too
many links, but you may also find yourself with leaf categories that contain only one or two items and this can create
the overall impression that your website has a poor range.
Imagine the above example broken down even further:

Clothing > Women's Clothing > Dresses > Dress Styles >
Brands > Sizes > Colour Shades > Exact Colours

You can see how quickly such choice could become over-
whelming to buyers.

Homework:

Check your competitors both online and
offline, and see how they choose to categorise
their items. Conduct an internet search for
products similar to yours to see how US and
UK websites categorise. Remember, they
often have years more experience operating
websites than Australians and can provide best
practice examples you should try to emulate.

2. *Relevant Merchandising*

As buyers spend more time online, and choose their favourite websites to return to repeatedly, a personalised experience is becoming an increasing demand. A personalised welcome note is nice to have; a friendly 'Welcome back, Todd' works for me, but in a more sophisticated way, the website that can show buyers those products of most interest to them personally, makes online shopping faster, more convenient and more pleasant. Merchandising can consist of how search results are returned, what products are featured on the homepage or other prominent areas of the site, what advertising buyers see (if any), what products and content appear in the emails they receive and what special offers, discounts or promotions they receive.

Outlined earlier in this chapter, the website that is built to be data enabled has all the ingredients to make a highly successful personalised shopping experience for each buyer. While it may not seem worth investing in this kind of functionality for a few hundred or a few thousand visitors to your site, you should always have the functionality in place so you can move to personalised recommendations at any stage in your business's growth. My advice is to do it from day one because every first visit to your website could very well be your only opportunity to gain a new customer and make them loyal. There are literally millions of websites and I know the products I sell are available on several other sites. Treating each of my customers as loyal and valued will be one of the ways I beat my competition.

Who's doing it well?

- Amazon, again, is world class at this. Every time I go to the website I have personal recommendations based not only on what I have searched for and purchased in the past, but also from what customers who share my interests have purchased. For every ten products they recommend, I am interested in at least 30–40 per cent of them and their recommendation engine has led to countless impulse buys from me in the past.

3. *Payment and Postage Options and Order Status*

Provide a dedicated page outlining which payment methods and postage options you provide, and (if applicable) how much each service costs. On this, or another dedicated page, you should have an area where buyers can check the status of their order: has payment been received; has the order been picked; has it left the warehouse; what method of postage/delivery was used; when can it be expected. More information about payment methods and logistics can be found in Chapters Four and Five.

4. *Customer Support and Help if Something Goes Wrong*

Online purchases can take place any time of the day or night, often while your staff members are tucked up in bed catching up on well-earned rest. While buyers may not generally expect or demand customer support availability 24 hours a day, seven days a week, clearly outline when you or your staff will be available to answer queries. Provide an estimated turnaround time for email enquiries and, if you are experiencing any delays, design your website in a way that allows you to message such delays to your customers. More of this, as well as the various options for customer support available for websites will be covered in Chapter Nine.

5. *About Your Business and Contact Details*

Buyers also expect a page that tells them more about your business. Remember that chances are high that this person knows little about your business before finding you online, and has almost certainly never visited your premises before, or met you in person. Tell them things like: how long you have been in business; who works with you; where you are located (a physical address instils more buyer confidence that your business is legitimate and you can be found if something goes wrong with the transaction); a phone number and an Australian Business Number (ABN) – all registered Australian businesses are required to display these in physical locations and should also do so online. If appropriate, show photos of your staff and your physical premises to help a buyer assess that you are a bona fide business.

Incorporate an online map service into your Contact Us details such as Google Maps or Bing. These are becoming minimum requirements for most websites today, and will also help improve your search engine optimisation (see Chapter Six).

6. *Coupons (the Extra Feature Buyers Love)*

Even if you do not intend offering them straightaway, you should definitely consider enabling your website for coupons. Coupons are virtual discount vouchers that can be offered across your entire range of products to all buyers, or on selected products to your most loyal and valuable customers. At some point, for example, you may want to email your buyer base with a special percentage off your products or services, as this will help bring buyers back to your website, spread positive word of mouth, and may even drive new buyers to your business. After price and service, the next thing buyers look for is a sense of being valued by your business – that they are special. While you could offer these types of discounts and manage them manually, planning to do this in a scalable way from day one will save you countless hours and potential buyer frustration in the future.

A word of warning – do not let coupons become the drug of choice for your buyers. They are highly addictive and may lead to unrealistic expectations from your customers that every purchase will be incentivised with a considerable discount. Use them selectively and meaningfully and seek to provide them with minimum purchase requirements (spend $20 or more to receive the discount). If you do not ever intend to offer your buyers coupons, find other ways to excite them and entice them back to your site with special add-ons with purchases, or exclusivity to new releases for a limited time.

CHAPTER SUMMARY

- You appreciate why having your own website is critical to the future success of your business

- You understand how much you need to spend on your website and the options available for having your website built

- You know the five business essentials to every website and ensure yours has each of them enabled

- You know the five things buyers most want to see on your website and ensure you have them enabled

4
Online Payment Options

Enabling your website for eCommerce transactions

WHAT THIS CHAPTER WILL COVER

- How to enable your website to accept online payments

- How to accept online payment using mechanisms such as PayPal and Paymate

- Incorporating credit payments into your website

- The pros and cons of accepting bank transfers

Accepting Payments for Online Transactions

We have now established that having your own website and enabling it for eCommerce transactions is an essential part of your online business strategy. I recently went to purchase items at a nice looking website from a company I know well, but once I had put my items into the shopping cart, rather than a smooth, automated checkout process, I received a notice asking me to call the company and read my credit card details over the phone to complete the sale. In today's age of identity theft, I quickly closed down the website and have not returned. Many companies have tried various ways to avoid incorporating payments into their site but none has been successful long-term eCommerce strategies. In this chapter, I outline four of the most common options, though there is a host of other alternatives which you can find by conducting an internet search. Make sure you read their user agreements and terms of trade thoroughly, and are fully aware of their fee rates and protection schemes before deciding to accept them as part of your web experience.

Instilling Confidence in your Buyers

Of course, accepting money online necessarily complicates your business somewhat and introduces an element of risk. This risk can be easily managed by you, and fears over security concerns can be allayed for your buyers. Remember that a customer may be buying a product they have never seen from you (a company they have never heard of or been to) and in order to do so they need to send you funds. More often than not, they will want to do this electronically. You should spell out to your buyers why you have chosen to accept the payment methods you have, what lengths your business goes to in order to protect financial information and, if you store it, how do you do so securely? Be aware that storing financial information has legal implications and you should check with your lawyer, accountant or business advisor on what requirements need to be met.

Consider using a service such as VeriSign (www.verisign. com.au), a widely recognised form of website security that helps increase buyer confidence. They provide a 'trust seal' that shows potential buyers your identity has been confirmed and your website has passed the malware scan. Malware is malicious software or website content that can compromise a user's security. At the time of writing, you can have the VeriSign seal applied to your website for a cost of $39 per month but check their website for more information.

Buyers tend to look for the payment methods they are most familiar with and these are the ones I outline below. However, an internet search will reveal scores of options available. Google Checkout (https://checkout.google. com/seller/) is an option that has failed to gain traction in Australia but should be considered if you want to expand into the US market. Buyers will soon tell you if they have a preferred payment method you are not accepting and, rather than try to accept many of them, keep the choice limited to your buyers' favourites. It goes without saying that for local businesses, the payment solution must accept payments in Australian dollars and this will narrow your options significantly. If you are considering others, look for ones that offer your business protection from fraudulent payments, and ones that do not charge buyers a premium to use.

PayPal (www.paypal.com.au)

PayPal is the online payment mechanism owned by eBay, and is one of the most common online payment methods used by buyers. According to a Nielsen report in late 2010, PayPal remains online buyers' preferred payment method ahead of other online payment mechanisms and credit cards. PayPal operates by allowing you to accept payments from buyers without seeing any of their personal financial information, or them seeing yours. Customers can pay via credit card, bank account, or positive PayPal balance, and transfers in most cases are instant. PayPal then alerts you to having received payment, and attaches that payment to a specific transaction. Refer to my book *How to Use eBay and PayPal* for more detailed information about accepting PayPal on eBay and your own website, but below is some general information on incorporating it into your website.

Why Consider Using PayPal?

- It's among the most common forms of online payment methods.
- More than 3 million online shoppers in Australia pay with PayPal accounts.
- Over 40 000 Australian businesses currently accept PayPal.
- Incorporating PayPal into your website is a relatively simple process and can be operational in a matter of hours.

PayPal proudly supports tens of thousands of Australian businesses and entrepreneurs. PayPal enables businesses to accept payments from customers both locally and around the world. At PayPal, we pride ourselves on providing a safe, secure and convenient payment solution for both our merchant partners and Australian consumers, giving online shoppers the confidence to shop safely and securely online.

Frerk-Malte Feller, former Managing Director, PayPal Australia

- PayPal is one of the few payment methods than can be easily utilised to accept payments from buyers in other countries.
- Its rates are competitive with credit card merchant rates, starting as low as 1.1 per cent and 30 cents per transaction, or 5 per cent and 5 cents per transaction for lower priced items.
- It accepts payments securely without buyers having to share their financial information, and without you having to share yours.
- Some businesses and transactions may qualify for PayPal Seller Protection, protecting against 'item not received' claims and fraudulent buyer activity.

- PayPal's mobile app (available at the iTunes store) and mCommerce functionality allow you to pay for any online item (where PayPal is accepted), anytime, anywhere. PayPal also has apps for Android and BlackBerry. More information can be found at www. paypal-australia.com.au/personal/pay-using-paypal/ buy-on-a-mobile.

How to Use PayPal – Top Tips

1. Make sure you register for a business account.
2. Regardless of your current volumes, register for large seller discounts – if you register once you do not need to register again and, when you reach the volume thresholds, your fee rates will automatically reduce.
3. Connect your PayPal account to an email address that reflects your brand and is easily accessible by your accounts receivable staff.
4. Restrict access to your PayPal account to only those staff who need to control the finances of the business.
5. Change your PayPal password monthly to help protect your account and ensure only current staff with password knowledge have access to the account.
6. Due to government legislation, if your business gets large enough, you will need to go through an identification verification process with PayPal – it's strongly advised to do this at the outset so you never have to experience delays or restrictions on your account. You may need to provide evidence such as

photocopies of your ABN certificate, driver's licence, etc.

7. If you have any questions about PayPal, do not hesitate to call them. Their staff members are friendly and knowledgeable and at times the website can be confusing so the phone is often your fastest path to resolution. The phone number is available on the site, after you log in.

8. Even if you do not have a website, but are selling handmade crafts online via Facebook or another general site, for example, PayPal allows you to create professional-looking invoices and send them to your buyers for instant, easy-to-identify payments.

9. If you're mostly selling low-value items and the 30 cents per transaction eats too much into your margin, apply for micropayments, which calculate a 5 per cent and 5 cents per transaction fee rate to all your sales. You can apply for this special fee rate on the site.

10. If you want to open your business to global opportunities, remember that PayPal allows your buyers to pay in over 20 currencies.

11. Speak to PayPal about being included in their regular marketing campaigns.

Who's doing it well?

- eCommerce-only merchants are pioneers of PayPal and were quick to accept it as a payment method, especially when eBay took ownership of it.
- DealsDirect (www.dealsdirect.com.au), OO (www.oo.com.au), The Nile (www.thenile.com.au) and EziBuy (www.ezibuy.com.au) all accept PayPal and it is fully integrated into their checkout systems.
- PayPal's mobile app is encouraging more traditional businesses to accept PayPal payments – you can now pay for your Event Cinemas movie tickets on the way to the cinema without having to line up in those annoying box office queues!

Paymate (www.paymate.com)

Paymate is an Australian-owned payment company that grew in popularity on eBay and is now accepted by websites throughout Australia, New Zealand and the US. Offering similar services to PayPal, Paymate can be used to accept credit card payments from buyers on eBay and your website and also offers currency exchange.

Why Consider Using Paymate?

- It provides a very similar service to PayPal, with fee rates starting at 1.7 per cent per transaction (larger businesses will attract a monthly fee of between $3.30 and $33). Note that eBay fees are charged at the higher rate of 2.4 per cent plus 50 cents per transaction.

- Buyers do not have to register with Paymate to use their service and some buyers prefer not to have to sign up for a payment mechanism.

- Paymate makes payments directly into your business's bank account – funds are not held by Paymate.

- It is easy and fast to integrate into your site.

How to Use Paymate – Top Tips

1. Once you've registered for your chosen account level, monitor your sales to ensure you are receiving the best fee rate. You can log on to the site to upgrade your account level at any time after registration.

2. For payments via your own website, you can elect to make the buyer pay the Paymate fees – however, buyers do not like to be slugged with additional upfront fees, so it is strongly recommended *not* to use this feature if you are serious about growing your online sales.

3. Note that where a buyer challenges a payment – claims an illegal use of their credit card or item not received, for example – Paymate charges $30 per enquiry. If choosing to accept Paymate, it would be sensible to

budget for a minimum number of these per month so you have the funds to pay this charge.

4. Consider incorporating the Paymate Express logo into your website, which allows buyers to pay without being registered members. Be sure to provide all of the details of the order to Paymate so the buyer is not forced to re-enter the information. Details for how to do this can be found on the Paymate website.

5. Sign up for Paymate mobile services so your business can be ready to accept mobile payments via Paymate immediately.

6. Be aware that in order to accept Paymate on eBay, you need to have at least ten feedback points from different buyers in the past six months. Feedback is left for you by buyers after each transaction.

7. Paymate does not allow buyers in the following categories to use its service: airlines, alcohol vendors, some charities, businesses engaged in outbound telemarketing or door-to-door sales, prepaid giftcards, services, tickets and travel agents. A full list can be found on its website under Unacceptable Business Categories.

Alipay (www.alipay.com)

Though its use is generally restricted to Alibaba and other sites within the Alibaba group, if you intend expanding your online business into Asia, you should consider accepting

Alipay as it is China's largest third party payment provider. Unlike other payment options, Alipay operates via escrow, which means that buyers' payments are held in trust and not delivered to the seller until the buyer has received the goods, and verified that they are happy with them. For this reason, it is considered one of the safest and most pro-buyer payment methods available.

Why Consider Using Alipay?

- It has more than 550 million registered users.
- It facilitates over 8.5 million transactions daily.
- More than 500 000 merchants accept Alipay.
- It is the biggest online payment mechanism globally, as measured by total value of transactions.
- It is the preferred payment method on Alibaba.com, and the China B2C/C2C website, Taobao.
- Only consider Alipay for your business if you plan to expand into the Asian market and optimise your website for Asian search engines, or appear on Asian marketplaces.

How to Use Alipay – Top Tips

1. It is difficult navigating your way around the Alipay website as most of it is in Chinese, and English translations are hard to find.
2. The best way to learn more about Alipay is to sign up to become a seller on Alibaba and follow the steps and tips at that website.

Accepting Credit Card Payments via Your Website

Most offline businesses speak to their financial institution about providing merchant credit card facilities for their physical business. However, incorporating credit card payments into online does not mean getting the details from your customer and manually entering their card details into your EFTPOS terminal. Doing so could contravene Australia's privacy laws so check with your lawyer or accountant.

If you're accepting credit cards, what buyers expect is that they will be able to enter their credit card details themselves during the checkout process, and have your website automatically verify and approve the payment. Most banks I've spoken with are keen to help their business customers get online and will more than likely have an eCommerce solution applicable for your business. Speak to your financial institution to see what services they offer.

Why Consider Using Credit Card Facilities?

- Payment mechanisms such as PayPal and Paymate do not allow buyers to use all credit cards to pay for items: American Express and Diner's Club card, for example, cannot be used. Having an online merchant credit card facility gives you the option of accepting credit cards other than Visa and MasterCard.
- As you process the payment, you have the opportunity to store your buyers' credit card information for future

visits, meaning they will not be required to enter it again, or checkout via PayPal or Paymate next time they pay for an item.

- Some banks have ready-made eCommerce solutions that help you get your business online, and accept payments quickly and effectively. See the Commonwealth Bank's eVolve (evolve.commbank. com.au) and NAB's Transact (www.nab.com.au/ nabtransact) or consult your financial institution for more details.

- Be aware that generally banks and other financial institutions do not offer protection schemes so you will be at risk of fraudulent credit card activity that is subject to charge-backs – the credit card holder disputes the payment and it is generally reversed in their favour, even though you may have already dispatched the goods or provided the service.

How to Accept Credit Card Payments – Top Tips

1. All banks do not have the same fees and benefits. Shop around the various big banks and smaller financial institutions to ensure you are getting the best possible merchant rate, and best add-on benefits to being that bank's customer (if applicable).

2. If you have an existing business, run a report to gauge which credit cards your customers most like to use. Consider only offering to accept the most popular credit cards used by your customers.

3. Do not charge surcharges for credit card payments. Buyers hate being slugged with a surcharge for the privilege of paying with their credit card. If you're not prepared to wear the fees charged by the credit card company, do not accept it. You're more likely to deter customers by charging them, than by refusing it altogether.

4. Where possible, consider utilising your financial institution's ready-made online packages so you can benefit from a full range of product features rather than only launching your website with credit card facilities – some banks offer these services free of charge to business customers.

Accepting Bank Transfers

While it may be true that accepting bank transfers is one of the cheapest payment methods available for both you and the buyer, you need to balance fee-free transactions with the cost of other business overheads like staff members' time. At this stage, there is no functionality to automatically incorporate a direct bank transfer from a consumer to a business during the checkout process. In essence, this would need to be done manually, where you provide the buyer with your business bank account details, the buyer logs on to their bank website (or visits a branch in person) and transfers the money directly into your account. It is true that some, generally more old-fashioned, online buyers like the perceived security of a bank transfer but the reality is that it will lead to considerably increased work for you and your team.

Why Consider Accepting Bank Transfers?

- They are free!
- Most banks provide for them and they can be done online or in a branch, so people who feel less secure transferring money online have a payment method they are comfortable with.

My advice is to not allow bank transfers, and this is why:

- It's a clunky manual payment process that most buyers find too much hassle to want to use.
- It is very difficult to keep track of payments received into your account. If you are selling 1000 items at $5 each and 20 people buy and pay $5 on the same day, knowing which payment came from which person is very difficult to ascertain. It is therefore crucial, if you do want to accept bank transfers, that you clearly state that the buyer must leave their name with the payment details, though this cannot be done if the payment is made at a branch.
- Most payments are not instant. Not only do you have to keep logging into your bank account to check if payment has been received, it generally takes up to five business days for it to be received by you, which means you have a very impatient buyer waiting to

receive their product or service. While it is beyond your control, the buyer may perceive that the delay is your fault and judge your business accordingly, telling their friends not to buy from you.

- If you're still unconvinced, give it a try to gauge just how much demand there is for it within your category, and time how long it takes you to track each payment and whether this is truly a cost saving or more of a cost to your business.

How to Accept Bank Transfers – Top Tips

1. You will need to display your business's bank account details to buyers on your website, or include them in your invoice.
2. Clearly outline the steps involved for buyers and note that it may take up to five days for payments to clear, and that this in turn may cause a delay in buyers receiving their products.
3. Insist that all bank transfers be clearly labelled with a product number, customer name, invoice number or other identifier to make it easier for your staff to connect each payment with individual transactions.
4. Consider providing links to the most popular online banking sites to make it easier for buyers to go to their account and log in to transfer funds.

CHAPTER SUMMARY

- You understand that incorporating a payment method into your website makes it eCommerce enabled, or transactional, and that the acceptance of payment should be automated and not manual.

- You appreciate the differences between PayPal and Paymate and have decided which of these you would consider adding to your website. An internet search can show other options.

- You have spoken to your financial institution about incorporating credit card details into your website and shopped around for the best deal for your business.

- You have considered the pros (it's free!) and cons (it's a real hassle) of accepting bank transfers as a payment method.

5

The Logistics of eCommerce

Making sure your buyers receive their goods on time, and in perfect condition

WHAT THIS CHAPTER WILL COVER

- The basics of logistics for eCommerce

- How to exceed buyer expectations

- The range of stock your website should include

- Options for outsourcing your logistics to third parties

- Options for delivering your products and tips for offering pick-up

- The benefits of offering free postage

- The importance of packaging in contributing to the buyer experience

- Returns and warranties – what buyers expect

What are Logistics for eCommerce?

Now that you know how to create your website, integrate it into third party marketplaces and accept payments, you're ready to start the eCommerce channel of your business. You could have the best website in the world, with the smartest functionality and the most popular payment methods, but unless you can deliver your products to your buyers efficiently and quickly, all of that groundwork will have been in vain. This chapter outlines some common considerations for making sure that you can meet and exceed buyer expectations. (If your business only provides services, some of the content in this chapter will not be applicable to you.)

It is absolutely critical that your eCommerce strategy includes a thoroughly researched and impeccably executed logistics plan. Logistics includes not only the storing of your products, but the picking, packaging and sending of your products to the right buyer in the fastest time, at the lowest price. This side of your business could take more time, and more careful planning, to implement effectively than even creating and launching your website. Let's begin by considering what your online shoppers expect from the best websites around the world.

> Every online retailer is a logistics company, whether they want to be or not. We are all moving physical goods, and ensuring this is done consistently well is fundamental to the success of the enterprise. The imperative is to automate as many functions as possible, and have a zealous approach to watching the detail.
>
> *Jethro Marks, Director, TheNile.com.au*

Exceeding Buyer Expectations

Because online shoppers have the opportunity to sample the experience of a countless number of global websites (including those of your direct competitors) without ever leaving their home and all with a few clicks of a mouse, often their expectations are higher than those of offline customers. Offline, driving from one side of the city to the other to hunt down the best bargains and best service is not a consideration for those other than the most diehard shopping enthusiasts. Online, though, the effort required to find great bargains with great service can be as simple as clicking on a different link within a Google search. If you want to provide the best service in the world, buyers expect you to:

- Never be out of stock. Only display on your website those items that are guaranteed to be on your warehouse shelves.

- Deliver items as quickly as possible; same day or overnight is unbeatable service, within two days is highly competitive. This means two things: you need to pick the order as quickly as possible, and have a delivery method that is always reliable.

- Offer a variety of delivery options – some buyers do not mind paying for a premium service or for additional insurance if it guarantees speed or security.

- Deliver for free if possible. Often the cost of delivery is the driver of choice for online shoppers: if you factor in free delivery from day one of your business plan, you will never be beaten on price for shipping.

- Offer tracked shipping, that is, allow buyers to see at what stage of the delivery process their order is at. This includes: order received; order packed; order left the warehouse; order in transit (where it is – on a truck or at a depot); order delivered to premises; order signed as received.

- Consider pick-up options: some buyers may be in a hurry, may be located close to your business, or may prefer the security of inspecting the item before paying for it. Offer pick-up but if you do, make sure the items are ready and waiting, your business has a designated pick-up area and your staff are professional and courteous.

- Use quality packaging and pack your products carefully and professionally. Choose packing materials that ensure your products remain undamaged in transit, are not like unlocking a bank vault to open (it happens more often than you think), are environmentally friendly (minimise the plastic) and are clearly and professionally branded.

- Offer a returns service: items should be able to be returned to you if they are faulty or damaged, or if buyers are dissatisfied with their purchase.
- Enable free returns – wherever possible, consider covering the cost of returning the goods to your warehouse. Though buyers need to pay for transport costs (petrol, train or bus fares, etc.) to return items to a physical store, they are generally not conscious of it. They want no additional cost of postage to return a product bought online.

Stock Availability

The most successful eCommerce retailers in the US and the UK are those that have a dedicated warehouse for their website stock. In Australia, retailers and small businesses alike often make the mistake of using their retail shop as the warehouse for their online business. This is a bad idea because:

- You're asking sales staff to become picking and packing staff (entirely different skills).
- You are paying high retail rent and other overheads for products that online consumers do not need to see merchandised in a retail store. (This increases your

online overhead costs and limits your ability to meet online price expectations.)

- Your web inventory system needs to be seamlessly integrated with your retail store point of sale so that your website is instantly and constantly updated with quantities available.
- The time it takes for staff in your back office to go and walk the shop floor to find the item, then remove it from its display and pack it for dispatch will generally be a lot longer than if you have a space specifically designed for the purpose and a system which avoids double and triple handling of the product.

Other businesses try to start their eCommerce strategy with a drop-ship arrangement with their suppliers or manufacturers. A drop-ship arrangement means you sell direct to the consumer but do not hold any stock, so once the order and payment have been received, you contact the supplier to send the product to you, or direct to the consumer. I have not yet witnessed a seamless drop-ship operation for the following reasons:

- The supplier runs out of stock and you do not get to update your online inventory before the buyer makes the purchase.
- Time delays between the buyer making the purchase, the supplier delivering the product to you, and you delivering the product to the buyer.

- The supplier that sends direct to the consumer may not have the best system in place and can send the wrong product, or volume of product, or else does not pack the item properly.
- The service offered by the supplier – who is used to working business to business, rather than business to consumer – is beyond your control, so your customer's ultimate happiness depends entirely on someone else.
- Licensing and regional limitations may apply to some suppliers dealing direct with consumers or allowing you to re-sell their products on third party websites – always ensure you have the brand owner's consent to do so.

The most effective solution to these issues is to have a wholesale operation dedicated to servicing your website. A less expensive location that is specifically engineered to process single and multiple quantity orders and dispatch to all areas within Australia (or globally), with experienced warehouse staff is crucial to long-term success. The premises needs to be professionally designed by a logistics expert, who can help you optimise space and efficiency and save you time and money. Even if you have only, say, 200 products for sale on your website, two orders per day can very quickly escalate to 2000 and if you do not have the foundations in place to handle this effectively you will waste time, and put you and your staff at risk of injury. For larger operations, consider consulting with an ergonomics expert. Always make sure your place of business conforms to Workplace and Occupational Health and Safety standards, and you have the correct insurance premiums in place. Your business advisor should be able to assist with these aspects of your business. Investing in the right logistics technology upfront will contribute to a more profitable and successful eCommerce strategy longer term.

The Range of Stock Online

I outlined in Chapter Three that your website should include your complete range of products or services for sale. It is worth repeating here the two main reasons why providing your complete inventory online is crucial to long-term eCommerce success:

1. Your existing (offline) customers expect that their online experience will mirror their instore experience. An initial visit to your website, if it provides a disappointingly limited selection of the range of products your company is known for, may result in a permanently lost online customer, and contribute to negative word of mouth about your online offering. If I have been buying 'product x' from you for years then I expect to see it on your website.

2. Online customers who are completely new to your business may not be aware that your offline store offers significantly more range than your website. Remember that online customers are price and convenience driven

so if they cannot find what they are looking for on your website, they will quickly find it somewhere else. Having a product sit in a physical store that receives 600 customers through its doors a day is failing to capitalise on the eight million Australians who shop online each year.

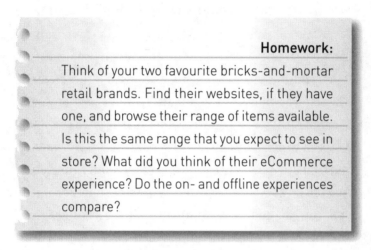

Homework:

Think of your two favourite bricks-and-mortar retail brands. Find their websites, if they have one, and browse their range of items available. Is this the same range that you expect to see in store? What did you think of their eCommerce experience? Do the on- and offline experiences compare?

Outsourcing Logistics

Some companies provide your business with the option of handling all logistics on your behalf. You simply deliver all of the products you have available online to the third party's warehouse, integrate your website's backend or else manually provide a list of orders and addressees, and the third party will handle the fulfilment for you. In Chapter Two, I outlined companies that can handle the entire end-to-end solution for you, including managing the sale and interaction with customers. In this instance, you still get to retain the customer and manage your own website, but do not have to worry about handling the products and getting them into the customers' hands.

Make sure you do some thorough research on the best options for your business, including minimum service standards, total costs, protections for your business and network coverage (where your products can, and cannot, be delivered). While most supply chain solution providers are geared toward bigger businesses and some do not handle business-to-consumer operations, internet research can help you find a solution that's right for your business. Australia Post's Post Logistics order management solution has been specifically designed for multi-channel businesses and includes warehousing and inventory control. In essence, Australia Post can manage every step of the supply chain for you. You can find more information at www.auspost.com. au/business/logistics-and-fulfillment.html. Big W, for example, utilises Australia Post for most of its online deliveries.

Delivery Options

You may have been operating a business for years now and think that you know all the options available for delivery but increasingly, delivery of online purchases is becoming a specialised skill. Unless you have investigated all providers with the specific task of fulfilling delivery of your online sales, you need to go back and invest some time in assessing all of the options available. This is also a constantly evolving space, and new technologies and solutions are regularly emerging in what is fast becoming a hotly contested service space. When weighing up which options are right for your business, compare costs (always look for discounts for higher volumes), capacity to handle the future growth of your business, coverage, business protection/loss prevention, the range of clients using the service and whether they provide testimonials, and whether there is the option to distribute internationally.

Using only one service provider may not necessarily be your best option. Some, for example, provide a flat rate regardless of where the parcel originates or is being sent to, while others offer a sliding scale, and some offer volume discounts. One provider might be your cheapest option for within your own state, while another provides more competitive rates for interstate delivery. Mix and match providers to get the best solution for your business's specific needs.

Some service providers to consider are:

1. **Temando** (www.temando.com) Essentially a shipping aggregator that does not offer delivery services itself. It is, however, one of the most effective starting points for your research into understanding which provider has the best solution for your business needs. Temando has website integration which allows you to give your buyers more choice for delivery and its partnerships with providers means that it can often negotiate cheaper rates on your behalf. It adds the option of

insurance for a nominal 1.1 per cent of the purchase price.

2. **Australia Post** (www.auspost.com.au) With Australia's largest number of drop-off locations, Australia Post's parcel business has become its focus over recent years. Speak to your local representative about pick-up options from your business and don't assume its off-the-shelf options are the only ones for your business.

3. **DHL** (www.dhl.com.au) As well as delivery services including tracked delivery, DHL offer warehousing and supply chain solutions.

4. **Australian Air Express** (www.aae.com.au) A partnership between Qantas and Australia Post that offers track and trace, and express services.

5. **Allied Express** (www.alliedexpress.com.au) Australia's largest independently owned courier and express freight company offering logistics solutions and local and national distribution.

6. **Pack & Send** (www.packsend.com.au) Provides total logistics solutions including a national network of drop-off locations, packaging materials, courier and freight services.

7. **Fastway Couriers** (www.fastway.com.au) Offers same-day and next-day courier services Australia wide, as well as international services.

8. **Quantium Solutions** (www.quantiumsolutions.com/au/) Offers warehousing, delivery, logistics and express services and operates in the Asia–Pacific region.

9. **TNT** (www.tnt.com.au) Offers truly global solutions, tracked deliveries and express options.

An internet search will help you find up to two hundred Australian companies, all vying for your online fulfilment business. Look for services with specific online solutions and, where possible, ask to visit their facilities so you can see first hand how they operate.

Larger businesses may also wish to consider operating outside of Australia. Some international postal and courier companies, due to economies of scale, are able to offer services and rates that are more competitive than locally based companies. Some of the businesses I have spoken to claim to be able to send items from international warehouses into Australia cheaper than domestic delivery providers. This will, of course, entail much more detailed research and considering establishing a foreign base for your business, but depending on the volume of sales you anticipate, this may be the most cost-effective solution for your business's distribution needs. Having your products stored overseas may also mean they qualify for GST-free importation. Australians do not have to pay GST on items under $1000 that are imported from overseas.

Whichever option you are considering, always be prepared to negotiate hard with your supplier, remaining realistic about the volumes your business is capable of; do not think that the advertised rates are the only option. More often than not, published rates are the most expensive and you can expect to work your way down from there.

Free Shipping

You will see that free shipping is a recurring theme throughout this book, because it is a frequently requested experience from online shoppers. Forcing buyers to pay for delivery only serves to create another reason why they should not be buying from you, or buying online at all. While buyers need to pay for transport to and from retail stores, parking costs, petrol, car wear and tear, or public transport, they generally don't consider these as additional costs for buying an item in the offline world. While you may be hesitant to include delivery for free, more and more of your competitors are doing so, and ignoring this will limit your ability to take market share in your particular category. Even some international retailers are delivering to Australia for free, which makes it very difficult for buyers to stomach paying for domestic delivery. There are two ways to offer free delivery:

1. Work out an average cost for delivery and then include this in the sale price for each item. This can work well for some online businesses but the price of items still needs to remain competitive. A general guide is that total cost must be less than recommended retail price.

2. Keep your product prices as they are, and absorb the postage costs yourself. This will reduce your margin,

but should significantly increase your sales volume.

If you manage this carefully, it should result in a larger profit.

If you're not convinced either strategy will work for you, or which will work best, use a marketplace like eBay to experiment. Keep everything identical in your listings, except the price. For one, offer it at the base price with free postage. On the second listing, offer it at the base price and charge for postage. On the third listing, offer it at a higher price with free postage. Watch what happens. Bear in mind that the results may vary by product so a uniform approach to your entire inventory may not work as well.

I recently made the change to free postage within my eBay store and my sales volume tripled. Even I was surprised by the results but the trade-off become a simple equation. It is better to sell 60 items at $2 profit per day ($120 total) than to sell 20 items at $4 profit ($80 total). Often, volume will be the driver of your eCommerce success, not preserving high margins.

Who's doing it well?

- Recently purchased by Amazon, The Book Depository (www.bookdepository.co.uk) offers free shipping, worldwide, all the time, and this is on top of significantly discounted books. It is understood that The Book Depository negotiated incredible deals with Royal Mail in the UK to be able to offer this service, though no details have been made public.
- Within Australia, The Nile (www.thenile. com.au) offers free shipping on all products Australia wide.

Homework:

Use Excel to design a simple business model that calculates what volume of products you would need to sell each week if you wanted to absorb the cost of postage but receive the same amount in profit. Is it achievable for your business?

Professional Packaging

You have launched your website, your customers are buying large volumes and you have the best logistics solution in place for your business. But when they receive their products, your buyers discover a flimsy plastic bag that has been torn in transit, or a re-used fruit and vegetable box that still smells like last week's dinner. This happens more frequently with online businesses than you would imagine. The way you package your online sales is a critical part of creating an overall experience for your buyers. Here are some key tips that should become the bare minimum you consider:

1. Strong packaging that protects the product from getting damaged, or being tampered with, is the key to success.
2. Branded packaging serves not only as a sensible brand awareness exercise; it also helps boost buyers' perception for how professional your business is.
3. The colours, materials and textures you choose all contribute to your overall branding, and businesses that do it well easily stand apart from their competitors.
4. Add a simple card or brochure about your business and its products.
5. Include suggestions for how to use the product, or any specific cleaning directions that should be followed.
6. Include a discount voucher for repeat purchase.
7. Don't forget a simple thank you note.

The package should include anything that sales staff in a traditional retail store would be responsible for.

Who's doing it well?

- They are a fairly small company and their products are high quality and therefore quite expensive, but Bison (www.bisonhome.com.au) does a stand-out job packaging their items – well branded, environmentally friendly, with care instructions and a complimentary branded hessian shopping bag all contribute to creating an overall experience that lives up to their premium brand image.
- Whether you're buying a heavy appliance or delicate glassware, Peter's of Kensington (www.petersofkensington.com.au) always takes care to ensure their products remain in perfect condition.
- Huggies Bookclub (www.huggiesbookclub.com.au) emulates Amazon and sends books in tough cardboard pouches.

Returns and Warranties

When buyers purchase your items online, more often than not, they are purchasing a product they have never seen before. It may be an article of clothing they have not tried on, an ornament or trinket for the home, manchester . . . Whatever it is you are selling, it is extremely unlikely that the online display of the product is able to reproduce it in the exact way the naked eye can see it. When a buyer receives the item, the colour may be slightly different, the texture unexpected, or the size not accurate. In the offline world, buyers get a chance to touch, feel and try on products whereas in the online world this is generally impossible. However, offering buyers uncomplicated and hassle-free returns is one way to boost confidence, and help spread positive word of mouth about your business.

Have a clear and simple returns policy for your items and clearly outline who is responsible for paying return postage/shipping fees. Wherever possible, offer your buyers a minimum of a 30-day returns policy and cover the return costs yourself. In the retail world, sensible business models budget for something known as 'shrinkage' to cover theft, goods damaged in store, or goods returned by buyers and unable to be re-sold. For eCommerce, shrinkage should include items lost or damaged in transit, the cost of return postage and items unable to be re-sold once they have been returned. A minimum you should budget for is around 5 per cent and speak to your suppliers about helping to cover the cost of shrinkage for your online business.

Additional buyer confidence can come from a simple-to-understand warranty or guarantee. Warranties usually offer the buyer replacement goods or a refund in the event of a fault or damage, while a guarantee is usually a broader promise to the customer offering the same, as well as satisfaction with the product's use or performance. Either way, the buyer has an expectation that if they are unhappy with their purchase there is recourse for them.

Note that for some businesses, there are laws in place that mandate the provision of returns and/or warranties, so check with your business advisor or accountant. Some insurance policies will also help cover the costs of shrinkage or warranty costs.

Who's doing it well?

- Zappos (www.zappos.com), which was recently purchased by Amazon, is among the best in the business for returns. They not only accept returns for free, they actively encourage them. A fashion e-tailer, they advise their customers to buy multiple sizes and styles of clothes and try them on at home and simply return what they do not like or what does not fit – free of charge.

CHAPTER SUMMARY

- You understand what online shoppers consider to be best practice and try to include as many of these factors in your own website as possible.

- You understand that your website needs to list your entire inventory for sale.

- You have in place a logistics solution that never disappoints your customers, and helps maximise your profit by reducing overheads.

- You have investigated the options available for sending your products to buyers and have narrowed your choice to two or three providers who give you the best deal for your requirements.

- You have created a business model that allows you to offer your buyers free postage.

- You understand the importance of quality, branded packaging.

- Your business model has budgeted for shrinkage and the ability for buyers to return products to you – for free where possible.

6
Marketing and Advertising

Driving traffic to your website

WHAT THIS CHAPTER WILL COVER

- What search engine optimisation (SEO) is
- How to optimise your website for SEO to ensure it surfaces high in search results lists
- What search engine marketing (SEM) is
- Whether to advertise your website on search engines such as Google and Bing
- Advertising your website via other channels
- Shopping comparison websites to consider
- Affiliates programs and how they can play a role for your business
- Offline marketing for your website

Marketing and Advertising for your Website

You can have the best looking website in the world, with your entire range of products or services, and the best possible buyer experience, but all that you have invested will be wasted unless people can find you. It is true that any potential buyer will be able to find you simply by typing in your URL (or website address), but in reality that is only how a very small proportion of buyers shop online. Your most loyal customers should always be able to find you by going direct to your website, but what about the entire eight million Australians who shop online – or global customers?

It is worth pointing out here that your URL should be as close as possible to your business name. You should consider registering both the .com and .com.au address for your site as the .com name will help you secure a more global presence. Less popular addresses like .net or .org should be avoided – suffixes other than .com or .com.au are harder to remember and buyers should have instant recall of your URL. Avoid hyphens, ampersands or other symbols and avoid a mixture of numbers and letters, sticking purely to letters. Your URL should be your business name followed by .com.au, for example; and employ additional words like 'online', 'Australia' and the like if your most preferred URL is not available.

Having a successful mix of marketing and advertising as part of your eCommerce strategy is absolutely essential to your ongoing success as a business. Potential buyers should be able to find you when they search for a product or service that you sell. As with most channels you should consider, your marketing should be placed where your typical buyers will see it. If you're not sure how your customers are finding you, experiment with your online marketing and advertising strategy for a few months before locking in a medium-to long-term program designed to direct not simply traffic, but high-quality traffic, to your website. High quality here means customers who are looking for your products or service, and who are ready to purchase them now.

Homework:

Conduct a survey of your existing customers to see how they found your business, whether that is your physical location or your website. Consider conducting an online survey for website customers using a system such as Survey Monkey (www.surveymonkey. com) which allows you to create online surveys in minutes, often for free. Ensure you are complying with relevant privacy and spam legislation before conducting your research.

What is Search Engine Optimisation (SEO)?

SEO, also known as 'natural' or 'organic' search, is one of the buzz words of eCommerce. In fact, an entire cottage industry of boutique agencies has sprung up all over Australia (and the world) with the promise of helping your website appear higher in search results. Search engine optimisation is essentially 'free' online marketing, where your website appears in a search engine's (like Google or Bing) search result list, without you having to pay for it.

In essence, search engines send out 'bots' to trawl the world wide web looking for content that is relevant to the user's search. Bots have a specific way of understanding website content and the search engine applies an optimisation algorithm to decide where on the list your website should appear – more on that later. Websites are optimised, or given preferential placement, when the content is deemed to be highly relevant to what users are looking for. This can include a combination of text, images, videos and location, and it all depends on the way a search engine user interacts with their chosen engine, and what words they have entered into the search field.

SEO placements are generally not the first one or two results – these are usually banded or highlighted in some way – or in the right-hand column of the search results page, as both of these areas are reserved for paid search or SEM (search engine marketing – more on that below). All the other placements you see in the results list are a function of SEO. But how can you ensure that your website appears above your competitors', and where possible, at the very top of the list?

A robust SEO strategy is an essential part of any successful business strategy. Consumers are getting savvier and have more control in the purchase decision-making process – they search for relevant information online. With over 50 per cent of searches coming through organic (SEO) results, it's essential to optimise your website for search engines so that you're appearing in real-time, when your consumers are looking for you. Not only can a solid SEO strategy deliver an increase in customers and traffic to your site, but when implemented correctly, it can help you attract the right customers that have a life-time value to your brand. We regularly see a minimum of 30 per cent up to 350 per cent uplift in business results within three to six months.
Grace Chu, CEO, First Click Consulting

Optimising your Website for SEO

It is important to start this section by saying that only a select number of Google or Bing employees know the actual equation that drives their search engines' algorithms. As a website owner, you will never truly know the 100 per cent foolproof way of ensuring your website appears at the top of natural search. What's more, these algorithms are continually changing and where one day you may appear in position one, the very next you may be in position 101. Rather than trying to crack the code, there are a number of tightly held industry guidelines that will help your website remain in a favourable position in search results. Internet search engines also use differing algorithms so while you may be number one on the list at Bing, you might only achieve number eight on the list at Google. Most search engines also give you the opportunity to register your website to be included within their directory. It only takes a few minutes to do so, and might include a requirement to upload some new code within your website's backend, but it is well worth the effort to help ensure your site is being referenced. To submit your site to Bing go to www.bing.com/webmaster/submitsitepage.aspx and for Google go to www.google.com/webmasters.

While not exhaustive, and subject to change, the following tips serve as a great place to start, and the bare minimum that your website designer and copywriter should be aiming for. Bear in mind that after updating (or launching) your website, it will take around four to six weeks for the search engine bots to assess it for relevance.

Provide Clear and Relevant Tags

Every website has a set of tags, or meta tags, which is essentially a set of keywords to describe what your website is about. These keywords are one of the primary ways search engine bots decide whether your website is relevant for the search term that the user has entered into their search engine. The meta tags remain hidden from user view and are entered as part of your website's code. Only a designer or developer with access to your website's backend has access to change or update the keywords.

You can find most websites' tags by right clicking an area of the website and then clicking 'view source' or 'view code'. You can view both the meta description (a sentence or two about the content of the site) plus the meta keywords (a list of relevant search terms for your content). Good website designers and web developers know the importance of meta tags so make sure your chosen individual or agency is happy to talk to you about what you think should be included.

As a general guide, stick to highly relevant keywords and provide a list of common synonyms. Remember to be literal, and include variations of core words – for example, garden, gardens, gardener and gardening – to ensure you cover as many internet search variations as possible. Do not repeat a word as this will be seen as keyword spamming by search engine bots and your whole website may be ignored by them as a result. Keep your keywords focused on your products or services specifically, and your business name.

You can find tools at search engine websites that help you decide which keywords are the most relevant, and most searched, by users. Google Adwords, for example, shows a list of the most common searches for terms you enter. You can find the tool at https://adwords.google.com.au/select/KeywordToolExternal. Other sites such as eBay have tools that can show you the most common search terms from buyers as opposed to searchers (see www.terapeak.com for more information). Return to these tools every few months to ensure that your meta tags are updated to reflect the current most popularly entered search terms relating to your products and industry. Trends change and an outdated set of tags may mean that your website eventually falls in search ranking.

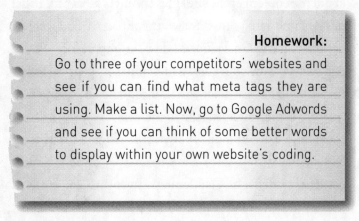

Homework:

Go to three of your competitors' websites and see if you can find what meta tags they are using. Make a list. Now, go to Google Adwords and see if you can think of some better words to display within your own website's coding.

Create a Website Title

Some websites also create a title within their code, which can often be viewed within an internet browser or tab. Give your website a logical, highly relevant title but keep it concise as buyers will be able to see it when they visit. Your title should be a descriptive sentence but no more than about five to ten words, depending on the length of each. Once your website is live, experiment with your title to decide not only what best describes your business, but also what looks the best to visitors to your site. Check it on a number of different internet browsers to make sure it appears effective across the most popular browsers.

Utilise Relevant, Keyword-Rich Text

The next most important area of your site to optimise for SEO is the actual website content. These are the words that buyers will see when they come to your site. Like tags, it is important to keep all the text on your site highly relevant, and utilise search tools like Google Adwords to make sure you are including as many popular words and synonyms as possible. Unlike tags, however, your website content, or copy, needs to be structured in the form of paragraphs and full sentences. A list of keywords that make no grammatical sense will likely be ignored by search engine bots, and don't think that making a list of keywords 'disappear' by writing them in white font on a white background will help either, as these tricks to try to circumvent the bots' view of relevance are quickly learnt and rejected by search engines.

Paragraph headings are very important to help define the content that follows. Your website designer or developer needs to label these as headings so the bots can read them as important text, not just words in the body of the content. Make sure your headings are descriptive but to the point. One word headings, such as 'Products', won't be highly relevant to an internet searcher (who ever searches for the term 'products'?) but then 'the world's best range of never-to-be-beaten bargain basement clothing' is not going to attract many searches either. Be factual and concise, and use the most popular keywords that your research reveals. 'Organic hemp shirts less than retail', for example, would be more relevant than the two previous examples.

Within your website copy, or content, keep paragraphs relatively brief – around 150 words or so. This will set out your content well for a better user experience, but will also help search engine bots quickly scan and process your content. Each sentence should, of course, be different and avoid repetition of common keywords and replace with synonyms instead.

Here is an example of what not to do, using website copy for a company called Harbour Hemp:

Products
Our shirts are the best shirts available online. Each shirt is made from quality hemp and is a shirt that will last you a lifetime. Try our shirts for yourself – once you try hemp, you'll never buy another shirt in any other material again.

And below is another example, one that is more likely to optimise SEO and place your website higher in relevance in a search results list.

Organic Hemp Shirts
Our range of hemp clothing includes locally designed shirts, T-shirts and tops to suit all weather. Hemp is the fibre cultivated from cannabis plants and ours is Australian grown on an organic farm on the North Coast of NSW. All

of our clothes are created to be fashionable, comfortable and durable. View our complete range of hemp shirts – all come with free delivery.

You can see that in this example, synonyms for shirts have been used, as well as broader terms such as clothes and clothing. A sentence about hemp has been included to cover searches for the material, rather than a specific type of clothing. Product features such as fashionable, comfortable and durable have been added, and the terms 'local', 'organic' and 'Australian grown' have been included for even broader search term coverage. Note the heading is concise at three prime keywords, while the term 'free delivery' is also included for searchers looking for this in particular.

Use Links Within, and To and From, your Website

Search engine bots like links. A keyword that is linked signifies that it is relevant and connected with more information relating to that term. I recently updated my author website – it was always surfacing at number three or four when you searched my name – so that wherever possible my name was linked to another area of my site, or to external sources. For me, that meant an author page at my publisher's website, or a review at a media site, etc. This tells the search engine bots that my website is rich with content about Todd Alexander and after making these changes, my website now appears first in search results thanks, in large part, to including more links.

Let's use the example above to show how we might use links to help optimise for SEO.

> *Organic Hemp Shirts[a]*
> *Our range of hemp clothing[b] includes locally designed shirts[c], T-shirts[d] and tops[e] to suit all weather. Hemp[f] is the fibre cultivated from cannabis plants and ours is Australian grown on an organic farm[g] on the North Coast of NSW. All of our clothes are created to be fashionable, comfortable and durable. View our complete range of hemp shirts[h] – all come with free delivery[i].*

Nine links have been included within this paragraph and here is where buyers will be sent if they click on any of the links.

(a) A search within the site showing all hemp shirts.

(b) A search within the site showing the entire clothing range.

(c) A list of all shirts for sale.

(d) A list of all T-shirts for sale.

(e) A list of all articles of clothing that are worn on the torso.

(f) A search within Wikipedia for the term 'hemp'.

(g) The homepage of the organic farm, whose website is also rich with content and ranks highly in search engines.

(h) A list of all shirts for sale.

(i) The paragraph within terms of trade outlining that
items receive free delivery.

Nine links within one paragraph is about the maximum you
would want to include. Bear in mind that this is an informational landing page on the website, not a product page.
Once buyers land on a product page, do not distract them
with links away from your products, or that all-important
'buy' button. Minimise links on these pages and keep links
restricted to informational pages to help optimise for SEO.
This should decrease the chances of visits to your site not
ending in a sale.

That is an example of how to link within your site, and
to external sites. You also need to find other websites that
can link to your site to help further increase relevance. This
could include links from Facebook or Twitter (see Chapter
Seven), from a website that hosts product reviews (write
these yourself, or ask your customers to), from an online
marketplace (some of them allow you to link to your own
website), from text advertisements (see later in this chapter)
or from sites that offer information about products like
yours, like Wikipedia.

Make sure that all of the links in your website are on keywords, not generic words. You should never link verbs like
'click here' or 'see' and other common links like 'About Us',
'Products', 'Gallery' and 'Contact Us' should be replaced with
links/tabs with terms such as 'About Harbour Hemp', 'Hemp

Clothing Range', 'Hemp Fashion' and 'Contact Harbour Hemp' to help optimise for SEO.

Where possible, use descriptive links for your category tree/taxonomy (see Chapter Three). Instead of 'size 6' as the link, use 'Hemp Shirts Size 6', but be conscious of how this appears to your buyers and if it looks too repetitive or text strings wrap on the screen, choose a better buyer experience over the small improvement in SEO that this would provide.

Use Text Instead of Images

You should definitely include as many images of your products as possible. When I refer to text instead of images, I am referring to the habit that some website designers and developers have of inserting a jpeg or gif image, for example, that reads 'Our Products' rather than having the actual text appear within the coding for the website. Search engine bots cannot read the text within the image, which is generally visible within code as 'img src'.

Make sure none of your important headings or product information text is loaded as an image (similar to word art within Microsoft Office programs) because, aside from the SEO implications, it takes web designers longer to create these images and therefore will cost you more to build your website if they use many of them.

SEO is a blend of art and science. It's about getting the critical technical elements right and blending it with the human element – communicating the right content to the right audiences. It takes an expert with skills spanning business, marketing and IT. To grow your business using SEO, there are four key levers that need to be integrated into your strategy: content, code, links and social. Having clear measurement and tracking in place to monitor performance over time is essential so you can benchmark and adjust strategy when necessary.

Grace Chu, CEO, First Click Consulting

Label Photographs, Videos and Images

When uploading photographs, videos or images to your website, make sure your web designer or developer labels these – most commonly, something called an 'alt tag' is used. Search engine bots are able to read these tags and therefore surface your images when a user conducts an image search within Google. Shopping by image is becoming a more popular way to shop online, and advancements in technology are making it possible for search engines to look for similar products based solely on their appearance. You may have noticed this type of technology in Facebook when you've uploaded a photograph and the platform suggests who the photograph is of. Clearly labelling all of your images with tags will make it easier for search engine bots to reference your products.

Incorporate Maps

Maps are becoming the vehicle that blurs the boundaries between online and offline transactions. They are therefore increasingly important for all Australian businesses, not just those with a website. Today, more and more customers are using internet or mobile map searches to find businesses close to their location. If you offer a service, or products that can be picked up in person, enabling customers to find you via a map search is very important.

Today, it's possible for a buyer to walk into one of your competitors' physical stores, use their phone to scan a product barcode and be instantly presented with a list of alternative places to find the product at a cheaper price, plus a map showing each business's location and its distance from their current location. If your business is not appearing in a map search, you may lose out on attracting some of these new customers. In Chapter Three I wrote that showing your online customers your physical address helps to instil buyer confidence that you are a trusted business; map functionality allows them to pinpoint your location precisely and adds further validity that you are a bona fide business.

Ensure your place of business is at least referenced by Google (www.google.com.au/intl/en/services) and Bing (www.microsoft.com/maps/developers/web.aspx).

Who's doing it well?

- Only you will be able to tell who is doing it well by conducting internet searches for products or services relevant to your business.
- Use a combination of your own knowledge and Google Adwords tools to run a number of searches and see which of your competitors frequently appear at the top of search results within the natural search area.
- Whichever competitor is appearing in the number one position for the widest range of relevant keyword searches is the business that is doing it best in your industry – it might even be you!

Search Engine Marketing (SEM)

SEM is the *other* industry buzzword and it basically means advertising – paying for ad placement – that directs traffic to your website. The most obvious channel for online advertising is with Google or another search engine, where, as mentioned previously, the text link to your website appears, sometimes shaded, at the very top of search results, or in a dedicated column, usually on the right-hand side. Most search engines ask you to pay per keyword so that your website can appear in ad spaces that are most relevant to what a user is searching for. This means you should have a complete list of keywords ordered from most relevant to your business to least relevant. You will more than likely need to bid for each keyword, and the business prepared to pay the highest amount per word will be the one that appears at the very top of the list. The more popular the keyword, the higher the price you will have to pay. On average, an effective SEM campaign may cost your business between 6 and 12 per cent of each sale.

All businesses should consider search marketing as efficient and cost-effective customer-led generation. On average, businesses pay a fraction of what they would normally invest in other major marketing channels, and only pay if customers click on their specific ads and links.
Ming Foong, Head of Search, Bing

Most search engines work on a cost-per-click basis. That is, you pay an amount for every click that sends a visitor to your website. Often these are called cost per click (CPC) or one thousand clicks. Another system that may be used is CPA (cost per acquired customer) or CPM (cost per impression – more on that later in this chapter). Bear in mind that when you are bidding for words, you may be competing with companies that have very deep online marketing pockets. eBay, for example, buys millions of keywords globally and is probably buying keywords to drive consumers direct to your eBay listings so you won't have to.

Not every single business needs to consider having a large SEM budget. If you have optimised your site well enough for SEO, and it frequently appears first in natural search lists for a whole range of keyword searches, you may find this drives sufficient traffic to your website. Before we look at the SEM options, there are some tips you should bear in mind:

- Do your research thoroughly to understand the most popularly searched keywords for your category or industry. Refer to the Google Adwords link provided earlier in this chapter.
- Use the most relevant page to link to your site, preferably one that is as few clicks away from the buyer completing a sale as possible.
- SEM placements include a limited number of words to lure buyers; continually experiment with your choice

and order of words to gauge which combination drives the most traffic.

- The most popular keywords are the most expensive but these will not always drive the best quality traffic to your website – make sure you measure clicks that lead to sales and work out a return on investment (ROI) that optimises sales, not just traffic.

- Continually try new things: new popular words may appear; more words may be required when you expand your range of products; highest performing keywords may deteriorate over time; so use the data that search engines provide (more on this below) to ensure the money you spend on SEM improves month on month.

Google

If you're reading this book, it is likely that Google (www.google.com.au) requires no introduction. Google has become a brand that is synonymous with the action of conducting an internet search, and is now a verb as well as a noun ('Google it'). In most English language markets (and others too), Google retains leadership on search engine activity. To have your website appear alongside other businesses in various placements across the web, you need to register for Google Adwords.

Why Consider Using Google Adwords?

- You can choose to have your ads appear not only on Google, but across a huge range of Google's network of partner sites.
- You can choose either text ads, or ads that appear in video (YouTube) and on mobile phones.
- Target your ads not only by keyword, but also by location of users and specific areas of the Google network including Google search, Gmail (Google's free email system) and other websites that your customers visit (eBay, for example).
- Google offers office hour telephone assistance on 1800 988 571.

Advertising on Google – Top Tips

1. Aim for high-quality advertisements: use Google's tools to help you identify the best and most reasonably priced keywords that relate to your business and its products or services.
2. Create campaigns centred on generic keywords to allow you to assess your performance in each and stick to one theme per campaign.
3. Carefully choose your matching options: a broad match will display your ad whenever your keywords or a variation of them are searched, whereas a negative match will *not* show your ad when a particular search is conducted. For example, your website will never appear

when a user enters certain keywords. This is effectively blocking your site from certain internet searches.

4. The text that appears beneath your ad can mean the difference between customers clicking on it, or not. Experiment with the text and where the link directs your customers, and run monthly reports to help you optimise your return on investment.

5. Keep your keywords and text specific to your products and use synonyms to broaden the appeal of your ads.

6. Review your Adwords statistics regularly (available after you create a campaign) to assess your clickthrough rate, the average position your ad appears and the first page bid cost (the cost of appearing on the first page) to see whether there is a way you can improve your ad's performance.

7. Download Google's helpful guide or watch the videos, which can be found at https://adwords.google.com.

Bing (www.bing.com.au)

Bing is the Microsoft-owned search engine that was launched in June 2009. By January 2011, Experian Hitwise reported that Bing had gained almost 13 per cent of global search traffic and as high as 30 per cent in the US. Bing is gradually taking market share from Google. Bing also powers the search at Yahoo!7 (http://au.yahoo.com).

Why Consider Using Bing?

- Bing has a highly effective picture search to help your customers find your products quickly.
- It is gaining share in a market that has long been dominated by Google. While Google is still the search engine leader, a proportion of your customers will be using Bing.
- As it is part of the Microsoft group, Bing is synonymous with searches wherever Office products are installed on a computer.

> Search engines are improving ways of providing solutions to consumers and simplifying the decision-making process. When users research a product, search engines like Bing are highlighting the ability for users to compare prices within search results pages instead of making them sieve through multiple websites.
>
> *Ming Foong, Head of Search, Bing*

Advertising on Bing – Top Tips

1. Use a combination of exact match, phrase match and broad match with the keywords you buy to help optimise your return on investment.

2. Use dynamic text, which automatically changes the copy associated with your ad depending on what the user has searched for.

3. Use intelligent targeting to serve your ads to the right customers, in the right locations.

4. View the editorial guidelines for tips on creating effective content at http://advertising.microsoft.com/ small-business/classroom-editorial-guidelines and also ensure that your ad conforms to Microsoft's policies.

5. Use the keyword research tool to help you choose the best words to include in your campaigns. The tool can be downloaded from http://advertising.microsoft.com.

Other Search Engines

As with most of the advice I give in this book, it is best to stick to the platforms that have the highest market share. You will generally end up paying more for appearing on a website that has the highest volume of traffic, but this is to be expected, and attempting to save a few pennies by appearing on a site with practically no traffic will soon reveal a poor return on investment. Be mindful of the fact that volume isn't the only factor that should determine whether your business uses a particular platform. It is also about quality. A website that drives three buyers to your business each day will always be more profitable than one that drives 10 000 visitors but only one buyer. While Google, Bing and Yahoo! are by far the most popular search engines in Australia, you may be able to find others that drive high-quality traffic to your website – keep experimenting and watch your budget's bottom line to decide which option is the best for attracting your specific customers. Never rest on your SEM laurels, but continually strive to improve your traffic volumes, buyer numbers and ROI.

Online Advertising, AKA Display Advertising

Another form of SEM is to utilise attractive graphics, or banners, to advertise your business on other websites and this is commonly known as display advertising. If you are a business that has an existing offline marketing budget, you may wish to consider incorporating an online component to your marketing mix. After all, what other form of advertising allows you to accurately measure the impact on your business, and create a direct connection between your advertisement and sales of your products or service?

Display advertising works similarly to SEM as outlined above. Instead of text links, however, you create a banner advertisement. You place this advertisement on your choice of websites, usually in a specific position across one or a number of pages and then pay the website host a fee. This will usually either be a CPC (or one thousand clicks), a CPM (or cost per impression, or one thousand impressions), which is basically each time someone lands on a page that displays your ad, or a CPA (cost per newly acquired customer). Often, businesses find that the cost of online advertising is significantly cheaper than launching another 'above the line' campaign like radio or television. The added bonus of measuring traffic that can be directly attributed to the advertisement means that calculating an indisputable ROI suddenly gets a lot easier.

Here are some basic tips to bear in mind when launching a display advertising campaign:

- Have your banner professionally designed by a web designer.
- Your brand and logo should be clearly identifiable.
- Keep the message simple and minimise text.
- Product images need to be clear and enticing: tiny images are a waste of space and a real turn-off for buyers.
- If using animation, keep it simple. Ask your designer to use a program that is fast to load and viewable by a majority of internet browsers.
- Provide a clear call to action, like '40 per cent off our entire range, one week only'.
- Spend some time actively looking at advertisements on other websites. What catches your eye and what do you think will attract the attention of your buyers?

To host your advertisement, choose a website that not only has high volumes of traffic, but one that can give you an indication of how successful banners on their site have been, that is, how many clicks they have received. Look for a host that can target your advertisement to a highly relevant audience, not just show it to every single person who comes to the site, and target your ad wherever possible to someone who is in the process of buying a product, or looking to buy. Aim for quality over quantity, so try for a CPC or CPA cost model instead of a CPM cost model. Finally, work with the host to receive as much data as possible so you can form a direct link between the advertisement and the type of customers you received, and what they went on to buy. Having a highly scientific campaign that is driven by data and numbers will generally give you the best ROI long term.

Here are some websites to consider for a display advertising campaign – they are ordered by highest volume of traffic according to www.alexa.com, at the time of writing:

1. **Facebook** (www.facebook.com) The social media website. It is estimated that 43 per cent of internet users visit the site each day. Audience has a female skew and more people access from home rather than work. See www.facebook.com/advertising for more information.

2. **YouTube** (www.youtube.com) The video sharing website. It is estimated that 30 per cent of internet users visit the site each day with over two billion videos viewed every day. Audience skew is toward 18–24-year-olds, slightly more female. See www.youtube.com/advertise for more information.

3. **Yahoo!** (www.yahoo.com.au) The portal and search provider has around 24 per cent of internet users visiting the site each day. Audience skew is

toward people 55+, and is slightly more female. See
au.advertising.yahoo.com for more information.

4. **eBay** (www.ebay.com.au) The world's largest online
   shopping site, it attracts around six million Australians
   each month. Audience tends to be strongly female
   skewed with 35–64-year-olds the stronger age group.
   See advertise.ebay.com.au/Home for more information.

5. **News** (www.news.com.au) News Limited's online
   portal covering a range of sites and informational
   pages with around six million visitors each month.
   The site has a male-skewed audience aged 35–64. See
   www.newsspace.com.au/digital for more information.

While most of these sites encourage you to buy direct from
their sales teams (refer to each site for more information),
there are online agencies that can help you negotiate better
deals, or sell you 'remnant' placements (cheaper areas of the
site that do not receive prime traffic). An internet search will
show you a wide variety of options but look for an agency
with a proven track record and clients that you recognise.
Speak to a range of agencies to scope out who is offering the
best deal, and who has the most robust data to highlight
their successes. Wherever possible, see if you can speak to
the clients themselves and ask whether they were happy
with both the performance of the agency, and the performance of their online advertising campaign.

Homework:

Go to some of the websites listed on the previous pages and use the site as if you were looking for a product, some entertainment or information. Now, go back to the site and pay particular attention to the advertisements that appear. Did you notice them the first time? Which ads attracted most of your attention? Which were the most annoying? Were the ads relevant to what you were looking for? Consider what type of ad would best represent your products or services to your existing and potential customers.

Shopping Comparison Websites

While shopping comparison websites are not as popular in Australia as they are in the US, they still provide a convenient way for shoppers to purchase items online. They work by comparing your entire online inventory with the inventories of others in your category and charging you for every click direct to your website, or every click that results in a successful sale. Rather than placing a banner or display advertisement on the site, you upload your entire product database via a backend tool provided by the site. Shopping comparison sites, in turn, work to have their websites appear high in search engine results and aim to attract as much buyer traffic as possible, that is, high-quality traffic of customers who want to purchase an item.

Buyers go to shopping comparison websites to help simplify their search for products online. Aggregators like these bring together competitors on one site and save buyers from having to go to each individual website to conduct their comparisons. Note that listing your products on some online marketplaces may mean that your products automatically appear on shopping comparison sites because the marketplace has chosen to pay for their placement without you having to share the cost. eBay, for example, subscribes some of its sellers' products for inclusion on Shopping.com and Google Shopping. The products I sell on eBay are included in Google Shopping; I do not pay any extra for this exposure and Google, at present, accounts for around 8 per cent of all traffic to my eBay store.

Here are some tips to consider before deciding which comparison site is the best one for your business:

- Look for a partner that charges you based on sales, not just clicks. This is a measure of the quality of traffic, not just volume.
- Upload your entire inventory or, if this proves too expensive, consider uploading just your most popular products.
- Look for a partner that has the technology to make uploading your inventory as easy as possible – it should be done relatively quickly via a CSV Excel file or other readily available program.

- Ensure your images and product descriptions are enticing, accurate and relevant.
- Integrate your branding strongly for all areas of the platform including search results pages as well as product landing pages.
- Look for a partner that can provide you with data to help you continually improve your clickthrough rates and/or ROI.
- As with online marketplaces, ensure you are price competitive, though not necesssarily the cheapest as price is most important on a shopping comparison site.
- If the platform has customer reviews on the products you sell, be prepared for the occasional negative review. Encourage more of your customers to leave product reviews.

Comparison shopping remains a significant source of sales for leading online retailers worldwide. The most successful use all the available feed components to display products as richly as possible. Lowest price is not everything and, much like search engines, it takes time to optimise campaigns to achieve sustained results.

Adam Shalagin, Country Director Australia, Shopping.com

In order of highest traffic volumes at the time of writing, the shopping comparison websites you should consider for your business are:

1. **Google Shopping** (www.google.com.au/prdhp) While not, strictly speaking, a shopping comparison website, Google recently launched Google Shopping, which looks, feels and acts exactly the same as other sites within this category. In essence, Google Shopping is a product search for all products available online, as referenced by Google search bots.

2. **Nine MSN Shopping** (http://shopping.ninemsn. com.au) Very similar in style and functionality to Google Shopping but with a more appealing visual display and recommendations for products.

3. **Getprice** (www.getprice.com.au) Australia's leading shopping comparison-only service, invested in by News Digital. Attracts around 1.3 million Australians each month. Also has a mobile application.

4. **Shopping** (http://au.shopping.com/) Founded in Israel (as DealTime.com) in 1998 and purchased by eBay in 2005. Offers similar services to Getprice. Attracts just over one million Australians each month. Also has a mobile application.

5. **Lasoo** (www.lasoo.com.au) Began in 2007 as an online aggregator for offline catalogues, today the site is a mixture of on- and offline price comparisons with some products available for purchase online. Attracts almost

one million Australians each month. Also has a mobile application.

Affiliate Programs

Affiliate programs work by you paying another website to direct traffic to yours. Some affiliates have managed to build multi-million dollar businesses out of redirecting traffic to websites. Depending on the affiliate, you may pay a cost per click or a cost per acquisition fee. With some affiliates, you can drive the negotiation by suggesting your preferred fee and they can choose to include your website, or not. Finding affiliates, and managing not only the relationship but also payments, can be a time-consuming process. For this reason, it is usually best to use an affiliate commission partner who will manage the outsourcing of your website's links on your behalf. The partner should optimise your investment for you, and ensure that you are not paying for low-quality traffic.

Here are some things to consider before deciding whether to incorporate affiliates into your online marketing program:

- If choosing the sites yourself, managing the relationship for optimal investment takes time, as does arranging monthly payments and measuring each campaign.

- If using a commission partner – they generally take a percentage of the commission you are prepared to pay – be sure to read their terms and conditions thoroughly.
- Make sure you have ultimate control over where your brand appears; you may not wish to have it appear at adult or gaming sites, for example.
- Continually strive for improvements to your ROI by mixing up which sites you appear on, which text or graphics you use, and which pages you link to within your site.

An internet search will produce a range of options. You may wish to consider joining an existing program or agreeing between your friends and business acquaintances to serve as affiliates for each other.

You may also wish to sign up for an affiliates program by including advertisements in your own website to make additional money. Make sure the placements do not distract buyers from purchasing your products, and aim for a program whose look and feel does not cheapen or lessen the impact of your website. The most popular form of advertisements to incorporate into your website is Google AdSense – more information can be found at www.google.com/adsense.

Offline Marketing

Never underestimate the importance of driving direct traffic to your site. Direct traffic occurs when a visitor types your

URL (or website address) directly into an internet browser, rather than using a search engine or clicking on a link in another website. Like natural search, direct traffic is completely free, but unlike natural search, you don't need to worry about complex search engine algorithms and optimising your site for SEO to make it work. Direct traffic works either through word of mouth or as a result of you building awareness of your website via offline marketing channels.

As outlined in Chapter Three, creating the right URL for your business is critical, especially when it comes to offline marketing. Users must be able to remember your website address, and enter it into their browser correctly. Complicated spelling, the use of symbols or numbers, and superfluous words will only frustrate your customers' ability to find you.

It may sound obvious, but if you want the eCommerce part of your business to be significant, you need to build awareness of your website at every given opportunity. It is surprising that a lot of retailers in Australia do not do this effectively, whereas many in the UK and the US actively encourage customers to shop online because of the potential for improved margins for the retailer. Here are some tips for where you should include your URL:

- All forms of advertising including radio, television, print and outdoor.
- All forms of business stationery including envelopes, letterheads, business cards, etc.

- Prominent places throughout your physical store if you have one, especially your front window and external signage.
- Receipts and invoices.
- Shopping bags, packaging, tape and other materials used to pack your products.
- On the products themselves, where possible.
- Staff uniforms.
- All paper-based directories including phone books, etc.
- Prominently on vehicles owned and operated by the business.
- All brochures, catalogues, books and other printed materials.
- On gift vouchers and gift cards.
- Thank you notes and with compliments slips.

In essence, wherever your business name appears, your URL should be right there with it. What's more, you should make it easier for people to use your website by including computer kiosks within your physical store, if you have one. Train your staff to refer people to your website to see your complete range and, rather than hand out business cards, tell people to do a Google search for your name if they want to find you.

Sending customers to your website needs to become a complete communications strategy and your website, for all intents and purposes, needs to become the first place people go to learn anything about your business.

Homework:

Over the next week or so, pay close attention to all of the businesses that you encounter. Which businesses did an outstanding job of promoting the awareness of their website by using offline channels like advertising, stationery or instore experiences? Why did their tactics work? What components of their marketing could you emulate to help boost awareness of your own website?

CHAPTER SUMMARY

- You have learnt the difference between SEO and SEM and how each can be utilised to drive traffic to your website

- You understand the basic elements of SEO and how to help ensure your website appears high in natural search results

- You understand the various options for SEM and have created a list of potential websites where your display advertising and/or product feeds can appear

- You understand the importance of offline marketing in driving direct traffic to your website

Interview with Ming Foong
Head of Search, Bing

What priority should search engine optimisation take in my overall business strategy?

A simple way to consider search engine optimisation (SEO) is to compare it to a listing within a directory. You would list your business in a phone book as an easy way for potential customers to find you. SEO is the same. In fact, businesses should pay more attention to SEO because today, an internet search is the preferred method of finding business information. The efficiency of simply typing in a query to get an instant answer without trawling through pages of alphabetically sorted listings has driven the consumer preference for online directories.

Apart from ensuring that the link to your website is ranked as highly as possible in the first page of search results, businesses should also pay attention to the information included within the listing, as well as the landing page that the listing will link to. It should contain all the relevant information in a clear and concise format for potential customers.

SEO needs to be top-of-mind when you are building your website and not an afterthought once your website is live. While creating your website, work out how you will engage your customer online, and the behaviours you are anticipating.

How are the lines between online and offline shopping blurring? What do businesses need to do to adapt?

Consumers are more internet savvy, more exposed to different technologies and channels as a way to get online. Consumers' purchasing behaviours are changing rapidly, from increasing time spent on online product research, brand engagement via business's websites to transacting and completing purchases online.

There are many schools of thought about how the synergy between online and offline shopping should operate. It is hardly a one-size-fits-all approach. Consider a strategy that complements on- with offline. An effective strategy will address opportunities like: increasing sales via easy online payment methods; reducing cost of sales; showcasing product range and depth; catering to customer needs. In Japan, for example, major retailers are encouraging shoppers to experience products in the store but then inspire them to complete the purchase online by offering incentives like free delivery or discounts.

Businesses can also use online channels as a way to build customer engagement through content-rich, or 'sticky' experiences. Products and brands in the Fast Moving Consumer Goods (FMCG) category often create dynamic online destinations to improve brand perception and affinity. This addresses the usually low consideration during the purchase cycle and sways consumer decisions before we even enter a store to purchase. A good example is the beer category, where pricing usually plays a major role in consumer purchase decision-making. The Tooheys Extra Dry website (www.tooheysextradry.com.au) creates a rich and dynamic environment for user engagement and sales are driven via this online brand affinity.

The first step is to determine what role each of the on- and offline channels will play for your own business.

What tips do you have for keeping your search strategy current? How do you optimise performance?

When one searches, one wants to find. The most important objective needs to be a business's find-ability. Businesses should pay attention not only to SEO but also to search engine marketing (SEM). As adoption of mobile and other devices continues to grow, the evolution of search will take another step-change. Ensuring your SEO and SEM campaigns pay attention to local relevance (local search) will be more important. Vertical search is also continuing to change. eBay (www.ebay.com.au) is an example of this, where users intend to find products from within one website rather than trawl the entire internet. Many online retailers are partnering with category aggregators to ensure that consumers can see and consider their product more easily. Expedia (www.expedia.com.au) works with different airlines to provide user benefits like fare comparison, cross-selling accommodation and offering discounts.

What will the future hold for search? Are there new technologies we should be preparing for?

Search will continue to evolve, not only driven by technology innovation but also influenced by changing consumer behaviour. In the future, search results may not surface as a list of options but a range of consumer considerations will be presented via multiple touch points, and completely customised to the individual. The search capability of indexing all the information available to content targeted to individual consumers will be a given.

7
Social Media

The role of social media sites in your eCommerce strategy

WHAT THIS CHAPTER WILL COVER

- What social media is and what role it should have in your eCommerce strategy
- How social media is changing the face of commerce
- The top social media sites in Australia and why you should consider having a profile in each
- Tips for creating effective social media campaigns

Social media sites can broadly be defined as websites where people go to interact and exchange information. They are, more or less, for the purpose of communicating. In recent years, social media sites like Myspace, then Facebook and now Twitter and Google+ have become incredible forces of nature, changing the way we behave and communicate, and introducing a whole new way of life for us to learn and adopt. Of the top twelve most visited websites by Australians, five are social media sites. For a while there, you weren't anyone unless you had a Facebook page and it was no coincidence that the fastest growing demographic on Facebook recently were the silver surfers – the over 55s. Everyone, it seemed, had something to say and what was more interesting was that others were genuinely interested in reading about it.

I recently appeared at a conference to discuss the role of social media in eCommerce and most of the attendees were convinced that having a Facebook page and a Twitter profile were essential components of an effective eCommerce strategy. There were some members of the panel who felt that having a social media presence was vital whereas my view is that though social media is important, there are more pressing parts of your eCommerce strategy, with greater impact on your sales, that should be prioritised.

At the end of the day, whatever channel you choose to employ as part of your eCommerce strategy, the ultimate goal needs to result in sales. While every single person I know seems to be on Facebook, and about half are on Twitter, the vast majority of users are not looking to purchase a product or a service when they use these sites – they are generally looking to communicate or exchange information. You are much more likely to find a buyer on a transactional site like eBay, or in someone conducting a product search on Google, than you are in someone who is posting photographs on Facebook.

Having said that, social media is a continually evolving space. There is definitely a role for it in today's eCommerce strategy and there is likely to be a more important role for it to play in tomorrow's. Don't fall into the trap of thinking that social media can replace any other form of marketing (at least, not yet) as those worldwide social media phenomena that make stars from nobodies or turn your website into an instant success are difficult to achieve and impossible to predict. Word of mouth is something a business can try to encourage, but can never entirely control.

The Future of Social Networking

It is widely believed by the online community that social networking will become a significant driving force in the way buyers shop online. Imagine you are a seller of dresses. One of your customers appears in the background of a photograph uploaded to Facebook and someone sees the woman in the dress, likes the way it looks and wants to buy it. The user can click on the dress, enter their size and payment details and an order will automatically be sent to your website to be filled. This technology already exists, now it is just a question of when, and how, sites like Facebook integrate it into the user experience. This is just one example of how eCommerce can be impacted by social media sites. Social media can play a role beyond traditional marketing of your products or services. The smartest social media strategies employ various channels for a range of business benefits. These include:

- Interacting with your customers – fielding complaints, gathering new product or service ideas.
- Providing like-minded customers with a forum to exchange comments and ideas.
- Giving expert advice on technical and other product aspects (such as cleaning, styling, widest range of uses etc.).
- Updating customers on the latest trends within your industry and/or changes within your business (such as trading hours, website updates, new store openings etc.).
- Announcing the release of new products or services.
- Utilising existing blogs, forums and other discussions to increase awareness of your business or its products and services.
- Announcing sales, competitions, special events and prize draws to help keep your customers engaged.

The only limit to using social media sites are each site's policies, and your own imagination. Test different strategies to see which is the most effective for your business and always balance the time invested with the return (or direct impact on sales).

Effective Social Media Marketing

Businesses that are using social media marketing effectively are limiting the time they spend creating content, and focusing on generating loyalty for their brand and/or their products or services. It is vital to remember that all social media sites are public forums – just like on your website, every single thing you upload, or write, could be viewed by any member of the public, which includes your customers, competitors, journalists and the police. As a general rule, only write what you would be happy to see on the front page of a newspaper and never write anything negative, derogatory or potentially slanderous about anyone else. Zealous customers and online influencers can take written information from you or your employees and blast it all over the internet in seconds. As with all written information or opinions from your business, think very carefully about the tone you use, and the words you choose because negatively received comments can often be shared among social media users. All businesses want to avoid situations such as the one faced by Gasp in late 2011.[6] If your staff members have personal social media accounts, create an employee policy that clearly states they cannot write anything that connects them with your company or its products or services. As the business owner, it is critical that you retain control of how your business is presented within social media.

Your social media profiles or comments should always have a clear link to your website and the products or services you have for sale. Remember that your primary objective for a social media marketing strategy is to increase sales, so your products, and the ability to purchase them, should always feature prominently in anything that you do.

Try not to obsess about any negativity posted by consumers about your business or its products or services. In this age of instant social commentary you will never be able to ensure that everything written about you is positive. Expect to see honest and often critical reviews of your business and take them in the spirit they are intended – direct feedback from your customers that you can choose to listen to, or ignore. In fact, the best social media strategies utilise public forums to help redress negative customer experiences. Show all your customers and potential customers what you will do to engage with unhappy customers and help turn around their opinions. Often, your most loyal and vocal customers can help do this for you by providing independent and balanced commentary around your services or products and helping disgruntled customers see the positive traits of your business. More often than not, a public debate about your business, with some subtle guidance from a communications expert, will help resolve most issues before they become major. This form of influencing customers is free, and what better way to hear what both happy *and* unhappy customers say about your business, giving you the ideal opportunity to fix systems or processes that lead to negative experiences.

While it is free to join Twitter, Facebook and most other social networking sites, because they have such high traffic volumes, often businesses fall into the trap of creating an ad hoc social media strategy and either giving responsibility to multiple staff members, or to someone who does not possess the right experience or skills. Effective social media requires a significant investment in time, and could amount to anywhere between 25 and 100 per cent of one staff member's time. Always allocate your social media execution to someone who is from a marketing or communications background, and give them clear guidelines on how you want your business to be represented. When you consider this time investment, salary costs of social media could be anywhere from $10000 to $150000 so make sure that you are able to see tangible benefits from your campaigns or consider investing this money elsewhere in your business where the impact on sales is more measurable.

Facebook (www.facebook.com)

Facebook is the current phenomenon of online. Over the course of a few years, it managed to burst onto the scene and take significant market share of the time people spent online. Almost everyone we know is on Facebook, and using it weekly, if not daily, spending countless hours on the site to communicate with friends, or follow others. In turn, Facebook has become the subject of countless news articles, books, television documentaries, acquisition attempts and even a movie and, like Google, the term 'Facebook' has become a way of being, not just a website. Today, the site is estimated to be worth more than $50 billion.

While Facebook remains predominantly a site for individuals to exchange information, industry pundits predict that it will soon become central to the way consumers buy online. The question is whether it makes sense for your business to have a Facebook page, and what role that might serve in your long-term eCommerce strategy.

If you intend to launch a Facebook page for your business, set a very clear objective. It could be one, or a combination, of the following: building brand awareness and loyalty; an informational page on products and services; a place for like-minded customers to interact (with or without your mediation); a place for customers to communicate with staff and get advice or answers, etc.

Other businesses use Facebook pages to generally engage with customers by creating a dynamic, fun and interactive area where customers expect to be entertained, taught new things and treated like valuable components of the business's success.

Why Consider Using Facebook?

- How many people do you know who do *not* have a Facebook profile?
- The site is continually releasing new technology that inches it toward a transactional, eCommerce gateway.
- It is by far the most popular social media site on the internet with around 43 per cent of all users visiting the site daily.

Marketing on Facebook – Top Tips

1. Update your page regularly, at least weekly. Stagnant pages will soon lose favour with Facebook users and may result in customers no longer liking, visiting or connecting with your page. Release relevant and concise information that will appeal to customers.

2. Use your Facebook page to attract customers by offering exclusive discounts, invitations or specials. Give people a reason to want to Like your page, and to tell their friends about it. Be aware of Facebook's rules regarding promotion – you may find your account restricted or suspended if you breach a policy around incentive-based activities.

3. Keep your brand prominent. The tone of language, product pictures, page layout and style utilised should be a clear reflection of your brand.

4. Choose to Like/become friends with key influencers in your industry. This way, your customers who Like their page may see your profile and choose to also view and Like yours.

5. Include Facebook Like links on your website's product pages so users can share their favourite products with friends.

Who's doing it well?

- Qantas (www.facebook.com/Qantas) is a good example of a company using Facebook to release information to the public around news, events and sponsorships to build better brand affiliation; 100 000+ people like the page.
- Domino's (www.facebook.com/ DominosAustralia) is a strongly branded page, and one that offers daily deals and discounts to people who Like the page. It drives traffic to order pizza online and join its online club; 250 000+ people like the page.

Google+ (https://plus.google.com)

Google+ is a platform that has been launched to rival Facebook. Google+ gives users more control over their interactions with other users, by allocating 'circles' of groups. This way, you might choose to have one group of contacts who are your peers and industry professionals, another who are your suppliers, a third group for staff members and a final one for consumers. You can elect to show each group different information or, if you like, instead of managing multiple Facebook profiles, manage just one Google+ profile.

Until Google+ gains more traction in the Australian market, you may wish to consider experimenting with it but maintain Facebook as your primary social media page. Remember that it is most crucial to appear where the majority of your customers are.

Why Consider Using Google+?

- It gives you more control over which followers see what type of information you are publishing.
- As Google is the dominant search engine in Australia, the company is attempting to become dominant in other areas of web use. In the future, Google could become the one portal where the majority of internet users search, shop, interact via social media, share videos and photos, blog . . . the list goes on. Creating a Google+ presence now may mean that your business is more comprehensively integrated into Google's entire internet strategy in the future.
- Users of Google+ receive Sparks, which are websites that may appeal to them based on their user history. This means your business may be promoted to new customers via Google+.

Marketing on Google+ – Top Tips

1. Create your circles carefully and be particular about which contacts you allocate to each.
2. Keep your branding prominent and closely aligned with your website.

3. Incorporate Google+ links on your website's product pages to allow users to add that product to their interests.

4. Consider using Hangouts to bring together a community of customers. You could also utilise these for buyer research on new products, or ideas your business is working on.

YouTube

YouTube is a video-sharing website that hosts videos to communicate and entertain, and is used by amateurs and professionals alike. The site is a cost-effective way to show your customers more about the services or products you have for sale. Any videos you have hosted on your website should also be posted on YouTube.

Why Consider Using YouTube?

- YouTube attracts 31 per cent of all internet users to its site each day.
- It is the web's leading video-sharing service and two billion videos are viewed each day.
- Hosting videos on this site rather than your own works in your business's favour, as videos on your own site might distract customers from the task at hand: purchasing from you as soon as possible.

Marketing on YouTube – Top Tips

1. Use watermarks or text at the end of your videos to direct consumers to your website.

2. Create a YouTube channel that collects all of your YouTube videos at one URL.

3. Your YouTube channel should be strongly branded and all of your text should use a tone that reflects the core values of your business.

4. Comment on other videos on the site to help build your channel's profile. Keep comments concise and interesting and never denigrate another user's videos, products, business or service.

Twitter

Twitter is a microblogging site where people follow the commentary of others. Account holders create short paragraphs or sentences of 140 characters (known as tweets) and post these to the site to be viewed by people who have chosen to follow them. While Twitter is frequently quoted as a site used by celebrities to communicate with their fans and the media, some companies use Twitter to announce new product releases, sales and promotions and other information that customers – both new and potential – may find appealing.

Businesses also use Twitter to interact directly with customers and provide customer service or breaking news. Customers post their own tweets posing questions directly to your business and this way, you can share answers and information with a broader audience instead of via one-to-one email or chat communications. Loyal and enthusiastic customers can then re-tweet this information to their own followers, creating effective word of mouth when the message is a positive one to share.

Why Consider Using Twitter?

- Around 10 per cent of all internet users visit Twitter each day.
- It is a great way for loyal brand followers to learn more about your business and products – there is a real sense of being the 'first to know' with Twitter. It is almost a 'premium' social media site where like-minded people come together to listen to opinion leaders in various fields.
- It's good to use for public reactions or comments relating to news or events pertinent to your industry.
- Tweets can generate hype or interest around new product releases or launches.

Marketing on Twitter – Top Tips

1. Try to tweet at least three times a week to keep your followers engaged.
2. Keep your business tweets interesting and factual, do not use them to express opinions or views on others.

3. Spell-check thoroughly: tweeting misspellings will create the impression that your business is unprofessional.

4. Carefully choose other people and businesses to follow on Twitter. This is often how your customers will find you on the site. Pick those who have relevance to your business, products or services and start with those who have a large number of followers.

5. Remember that once information is in the public domain it is beyond your control so only tweet information you would be happy for the whole world to know.

Who's doing it well?

- DealsDirect (@DealsDirect) tweet regularly to announce arrivals of new stock, discounts and clearance sales as well as competitions for regular followers.
- Yates Gardening (@JudyHorton_) use Australian gardening expert Judy Horton to tweet seasonal tips and advice for green thumbs nationwide, relating most tweets back to Yates products that will solve common gardening problems.

Blogs

Blogs are sites that publish short articles or essays by individuals or companies and are generally available for free to readers on the internet. There are a number of blogging sites that host peoples' blogs and these can be found by conducting an internet search. The most popular blog site in Australia is Google's Blogger (www.blogger.com), which attracts around 13 per cent of all internet users daily, closely followed by WordPress (www.wordpress.org). You can also blog directly on your own website so customers can make more of a connection with your business and your staff members.

Another global site to consider is Tumblr (www.tumblr. com) where you can share practically anything about your business including text, photos, links or videos, and you can do this from your computer, phone or email. Tumblr has over 11 billion posts on its site, with more than 30 million added every day.

Blogging can be big business in and of itself. Many bloggers have hundreds of thousands of followers via their own websites and blog sites, and professional bloggers are highly influential. Consider employing the services of a popular blogger with an existing large follower base to gain access to an instant customer base. Some business and public relations (PR) companies actively engage with bloggers to try to get them to share positive opinions about products or services. While some bloggers will do so in exchange for a fee or free products or services, other bloggers publicly criticise this practice and actively reject attempts to have their opinions bought. If you are considering seeking professional bloggers in your industry to help influence their followers about your products or services, never send chain or automated emails, always approach a blogger individually with a tailored proposal that gives a clear indication of why you specifically have chosen to contact them. A positive blog from a widely followed blogger can have direct, measurable and big impacts on your sales. Wherever possible, ensure that any blog about your company links back to your website.

Why Consider Using Blogs?

- They are a fast, easy and inexpensive way to communicate with your customers, and help build more loyalty with your brand and an affinity with your staff members.
- If your products or services are quite technical, a blog can be the most effective way of teaching customers how to use them effectively.
- Effective blogging can reduce your customer service contacts.

Marketing via Blogs – Top Tips

1. Clearly identify the author of the blog and their expertise. This gives readers a reason to respect the blogger's authority to share information about the given topic.

2. Ensure that your blog has direct links to your website and, if writing about a specific product or service, link directly to the relevant page on your site. This will assist with SEO (see Chapter Five).

3. Invite popular industry professionals to occasionally contribute to your blog to help build your blog's popularity.

4. Keep your posts informative, educational or entertaining – do not try to use your blog to market directly to your customers.

5. Allow customers to comment on your posts. Often a conversation between buyers will provide more interest for readers and help provide incentive for people to come back and read other posts.

6. Inject the blog with your business's brand and personality. Be careful to avoid personal commentary or too much personality unless your blogger is well known to the public.

LinkedIn

LinkedIn is the Facebook of business. It is a site where professionals create a profile of their experience and connect with past and current colleagues, and other industry contacts. Think of it as a massive database of the world's CVs. If for nothing else, your LinkedIn profile can lead to professional relationships with others in your industry, a way to exchange information and best practice that could help you improve your business.

Why Consider Using LinkedIn?

- It attracts around 5 per cent of all internet users each day.
- It has more than one million Australian members.
- It's less of a customer acquisition channel and more of an opportunity to network with other professionals in your field.

Marketing on LinkedIn – Top Tips

1. If looking for staff, use LinkedIn to find professionals with experience in your industry, or experience working with your competitors.
2. Keep your profile brief and accurate – it is a public record of your work experience.
3. Update your profile to reflect your current position and any news related to your company.
4. Subscribe to receive updates about your peers and other relevant industry news to build your knowledge of your industry and new local and global developments.
5. Remember that even global CEOs could be one of your customers so keep your profile professional and do not spam people with requests to be linked. Any request to someone who is a stranger, or who may not remember you, should come with a personal introduction and reason for wanting to link.

CHAPTER SUMMARY

- You understand what social media sites are and how they can be utilised by your business

- Your main objective with social media marketing is to generate incremental sales

- Your business needs to balance the time required to create effective social media campaigns with the direct, measurable impact on sales or brand loyalty

- You know the five most popular social media sites in Australia and how your business can optimise awareness for your website via each

8
Mobile Commerce

The changing face of commerce

WHAT YOU WILL LEARN IN THIS CHAPTER

- How mobile is changing the face of commerce
- The role of mCommerce in your eCommerce strategy
- How to build an effective mobile app
- Ensuring your business is indexed by third party mobile apps
- Accepting mobile payments

Thirty years ago, mobile phones barely existed. Twenty years ago, they were the size of standard landline phones and you might have had to attach an aerial to your car, or carry one around with you in a briefcase. Ten years ago, everyone had a mobile but they were more or less still telephones and had little additional functionality. Today, you can do so much on your mobile device – talk, write, see video, use the internet, take photos, store and play music, play games . . . Most importantly for your business, mobile is changing the face of commerce. Not all businesses may be aware of the mobile technology that enables users to:

- Scan product barcodes and be presented with a list of offline and online businesses to purchase the product from, and their asking price.
- Instantly search at shopping comparison sites.
- View a map showing the nearest business offering the products or services they are looking for.
- Upload photos to see how particular products will 'look' on customers. Customers can upload photographs of themselves and have your products super-imposed onto their image so they can see, virtually, your products against their face or body.
- Pay for goods and services without using credit cards or cash. Using mobile payment solutions such as PayPal, for example, customers can instantly transfer funds into your business account without needing to hand over cash or having their credit or EFTPOS card swiped.
- Receive an instant text message from nearby businesses offering local or short-term discounts.

All of this technology and much more already exists for mobile. Just imagine what tomorrow could look like, and how this will affect your customers and how they interact with your business. For eBay alone, more than 30 million people globally have downloaded its app, and more than $4 billion worth of goods was purchased via mobile in 2011. Australians are fast adopters of new technologies and in the not-too-distant future, more people will be accessing the internet, and buying online, from their mobile than they will from their desktop or laptop.

This could be great news for businesses – with consumers spending their down time when waiting for friends, on public transport or just relaxing in a park, using their mobile devices to spend money. At the same time, you can see how these developments blur the line between online and offline. Mobile drives both activities, with a particular emphasis on local offline. Your business needs to be referenced by mobile applications in order to attract buyers in your local area.

Mobile Applications (Apps)

Should your business have a mobile application? A mobile application is an interface specifically built for use on a mobile device. The application does not have to be the same as your website, in fact, it can be a more visually enticing and streamlined user experience designed to build customer loyalty to your brand, and drive sales. An internet search will reveal a host of agencies that can design an app for your business and the costs will range from a few thousand dollars to tens of thousands of dollars, depending on how sophisticated your design requirements are. Realistically, only larger Australian companies such as Woolworths or Coles are currently releasing apps for their businesses as consumers tend to favour apps that are broader than one business. If you are creating an app for your business, here are some tips to bear in mind:

- Include unique functionality that is better or more interactive than your website. If selling clothing, for example, consider allowing customers to upload their measurements so their clothing size is automatically calculated for them. Google recently announced that it would give preferential exposure to websites that were enabled for mCommerce in advertisements shown to mobile phone users.

- Keep your branding strong throughout the entire app experience.

- Make your products or services the heroes of the app. Employ crisp, modern photography and features such as a magnifier to help users see more detail.

- Your primary aim is to increase sales, so balance functionality with practicality – you need to make it as easy, and fast as possible for buyers to purchase their items.

- Regularly provide updates to your app and ensure you have a way to keep track of bugs that are reported by your customers.

- Give your app users a special incentive for continuing to use it. Consider offering discounts, virtual 'happy hour' sales, invitations to exclusive events or other rewards for being a loyal app user.

- Great apps can create strong advocates of your brand so invest accordingly and never release an app that has not been thoroughly tested, or is not a high-quality extension of your existing brand.

Who's doing it well?

- The Woolworths app allows you to choose your preferred local store and scan items from your pantry to automatically add to a shopping list that tells you where in the store you can find each item – pretty cool stuff!
- For lovers of fashion, the Net-a-Porter (US company) app provides a striking visual presentation of clothes that will have the most ardent offline shopper frothing at the mouth. The experience is smooth, fast and simple and lets the company's products do all the talking.

Third Party Apps

Rather than build your own mobile app, you also have the cheaper option of ensuring your business is included on the most popular apps available. A quick search of Apple's or other devices' app stores will show you what the most popular apps are. eBay, for example, is often one of the most

Who's doing it well?

- Telstra's Sensis WhereIs app allows users to find the location of, and directions to, the following types of businesses: post offices, restaurants, supermarkets, takeaways, parking and petrol stations, florists, doctors, cinemas, chemists, cafes, bars and accommodation.
- eBay's app will be responsible for around 10 per cent of all sales this year, which highlights how popular the app is, and how people use it to buy items anytime, anywhere.
- Group buying apps like Groupon's make sure you receive daily alerts on your phone for the latest deals in your area, and also have the added functionality of sending the voucher to your phone so there's no need to print vouchers or wait to receive them in the mail.

downloaded apps each week, and if your products appear on eBay, they will be able to appear on its mobile app. Similar apps are available for other online marketplaces, deal sites and shopping comparison sites.

Ensure the location of your business is indexed by Google and Bing maps (refer Chapter Five) and other mechanisms such as Telstra's Sensis WhereIs app (www.whereis.com).

Refer to app stores regularly to see which apps are the most popular downloads in the Australian marketplace. More often than not, the ones that might be relevant for your business are generic apps designed to help customers find, compare and rate businesses or products. If your business is not being referenced by the most popular apps, find their creators and follow guidelines for adding your business to their index.

Mobile Payments

Your business should already be equipped with the ability to accept mobile payments. This is particularly important in the online/offline blurred transaction, where a customer finds your business online but wants to come to you to see the product, and pay for it in person. In the not-too-distant future, customers may want to pay for all sorts of products and services using their mobile phone or other device, and if your business is not capable of receiving these types of payments you may lose that customer permanently. Wallets, cash and credit cards may become a thing of the past, as will plastic gift and loyalty cards. New software allows customers to pay for items by flashing their mobile device and often this transaction can be faster than using a credit card, or paying with cash. Fig Card (www.figcard.com) was recently purchased by eBay to make this a reality, and already Google has retaliated with its Google Wallet (www.google.com/wallet/). The space will be a hotly contended one, and with two internet giants competing for it, you can be assured that it is where they see the future of commerce heading. Be prepared to accept these payment mechanisms as soon as they become available in the Australian market.

PayPal's mobile payment mechanism already allows a customer to pay funds directly into your PayPal account simply by 'bumping' their mobile phone against yours, while the PayPal app allows customers to send you funds anytime, and from anywhere, by using a number of different funding sources ... no need to go to ATMs any more. Check with your payment service or financial institution to see whether apps are available for mobile payment solutions.

CHAPTER SUMMARY

- You understand that mobile devices are changing, and will continue to change, the way customers shop

- You know the different smart phone devices and how they allow customers to interact with your website

- You know the tips to creating your own successful mobile app

- You appreciate that third party apps may be a more cost-effective way to be found via mobile, and need to ensure your business is being indexed by the most popular ones

- You understand the importance of being able to accept mobile payments

9

Online Customer Service

The online customer

WHAT THIS CHAPTER WILL COVER

- How online customers are different from face-to-face customers

- What your minimum online customer service standards should be

- The various options for online customer support and which will be the most appropriate for your business

---

If someone is purchasing from you online, it is more than likely that they are spending their money on a product they have never seen, with someone they have never met. Online customers are required to invest a high degree of trust in online businesses and have expectations that may be different from those who choose a face-to-face transaction. Online customers are also predominantly driven by price. In its report, *The Rise and Rise of Online Retail*,[7] the Australia Institute found that 85 per cent of respondents went online in order to save money. While it may be perceived that online comes with an accompanying 'trust discount' – a trade-off between security and price – the website that offers customers outstanding service and secure peace of mind is the website that consumers will choose to return to, time after time.

In Chapters Five and Six, I covered how your website can promote trust in buyers, and deliver outstanding service via a comprehensive logistics solution. In this chapter, I will cover the various methods of customer service that you should consider for your website.

Great Customer Support – Critical Elements of Success

- Customers need to be able to find your customer support team quickly. Prominently display your Contact Us link at multiple points throughout the site.
- Training your customer service representatives is arguably the most important factor in keeping your customers happy – offer extensive and comprehensive training for your agents, and regularly update their knowledge base as your business evolves.
- Your customer service should be tracked. Develop surveys for customers to complete; these should measure satisfaction with the contact system chosen, speed of response, performance of the agent and whether the customer's issue was resolved.
- Make sure your customer service agents feel a valued part of your team. Often they will be among the lowest

paid members of staff, but as the 'face' of your business, they should also be considered among your most important.

- Set minimum service standards and provide incentives and rewards for agents who exceed them.
- As the business owner or decision maker, it is critical that you allocate some time each year to sit with your agents and listen to, or watch, interactions with your customers – you may learn more about your business doing this than from even the most sophisticated spreadsheet.
- Ensure your agents have the ability to capture frequently occurring customer issues and fix them as soon as possible.
- Remember that any communication from your customer support team (or any staff member) is on the public record as representing your business's position.

The best websites offer a range of customer service contact options because different customers prefer different methods. Following are common options worth considering for your business.

Australia v Offshore

If your website experiences enough traffic, and high volumes of customer support requests, you may want to consider outsourcing your customer support function. The question then becomes whether it should be outsourced to an agency within Australia or one overseas. Most agencies located in Asia will provide more competitive rates than local ones, depending on your business's requirements. If you are thinking about hosting your customer support team offshore, here are some points to consider:

- Look for an agency with high-profile clients and, where possible, ask to speak to the clients to assess how happy they are with the performance of the agency.

- Factor into your budget a number of visits to the offshore agency; not only will you need to assist with training, but the more your staff visit the agency to make them understand your business strategy and philosophy, the better they will be able to incorporate it into their contacts with your customers.

- Set clear, measurable targets for your agency with regular meetings to assess progress.

- Have clear clauses within your contract that allow you to stop using the agency if it falls below agreed service levels.

- Regularly changing your agency is disruptive to your customers and staff and will cost you a significant amount of time and money.

- Agencies located in other countries may not be in the same time zone as Australia. Generally, staff forced to work late or early shifts are not as motivated or engaged as standard-office-hour staff, so bear this in mind when choosing your agency's location.

Australian customers are quite used to dealing with customer support staff based in foreign countries. While most agencies train their staff in Australian customs and culture, avoid agencies that attempt to mimic the Australian accent or colloquialisms and aim for a highly professional agency where differing accents are compensated by accurate and concise responses.

Telephone Support

It may sound illogical to consider offering telephone support for an online experience, but increasingly, online shoppers are looking for an overall experience that rivals bricks-and-mortar retail. This means that having someone to talk to, and ask questions of, a 'real person' and not some automated response, is becoming a high priority for buyers. As a bare minimum, you should offer telephone assistance during office hours. Your phone operators need to be professional customer service representatives who are well versed in your online experience, and who have a thorough knowledge of all products available for sale online. They should also know your logistics solutions and have access to backend systems to show them order progress, payment status and delivery status of every item purchased online.

Depending on the training you provide, and the knowledge and demeanour of your agents, telephone support tends to have the highest satisfaction rate for customers, as measured by whether their issue was resolved within the one communication.

Your telephone support system needs to offer a minimum standard of service such as:

- Giving an indication to customers of how long they should expect to wait to have their call answered.
- Employing some automation so the customer can choose options that direct their call to the most appropriate staff member.
- Providing an option for customers to leave their details and have a staff member call them back, if waiting times are long.
- Avoiding loud, annoying or repetitive music.
- If using recorded hold content, giving buyers more information about your business and the products you sell.
- Ensuring that operators are able to identify whether the customer is an online customer – consider a dedicated number for website transactions.
- Offering customers the option of entering their order or customer number (or similar) while they wait so your agents can view all the information before answering the call.
- Offering a toll-free number so customers Australia wide pay the price of a local call.
- Response times of no more than three to five minutes.

Video Support

The next best thing to face-to-face customer support is video support. Most computers and mobile phones are now equipped with small cameras that allow video communication. While the adoption of video support is relatively low among Australian companies, giving your customers the ability to see your staff will increase the amount of trust they place in your business, and will help your support staff build a faster rapport with customers.

If using video support, ensure that the customer support team is in a clean, attractive environment – you don't want your customers being able to see rubbish, piles of boxes or an inappropriate poster or display behind your agents. Systems such as Skype allow you to use video communications for free, in some areas. Skype (www.skype.com) is a voice over internet protocol (VOIP) technology allowing people to communicate via text, voice or video over the internet. More than 15 million people are on Skype at any given time.

Live Chat

Live chat is an online ask-and-answer tool that allows customers to interact instantly with service agents; programs such as Skype and Microsoft Messenger are popular examples. In these, a customer types questions to your customer support agents and receives a real-time response from the agent. Consider offering this service during business hours, but also extend to after-hours service. Software can assist your agents with cut-and-paste answers to frequently asked questions, but make sure your stored responses have been written by a professional and thoroughly spell-checked, and

can be inserted in the flow of real-time written communication without sounding clunky.

The ideal response time should be no more than one to
two minutes. Live chat tends to have the second highest
satisfaction rate for customers.

Virtual Agents

Virtual agents are like live chat, except that there is no agent
on the other end of the conversation – it is a computerised
set of answers to commonly asked questions. These systems
work based on keywords: when a customer enters a question
that contains a specific keyword, answers relating to that
specific word are offered to the customer. The effectiveness
of virtual agents depends entirely upon the quality of information entered in the backend, and the choice of keywords
that answers are provided to. Most of us have experienced
these, and they can often be more frustrating than satisfac-
tory. Do your research thoroughly before you decide which
system would work best for your business, and employ a
dedicated copywriter to upload the automated responses.
Ensure your database of information is constantly up to
date.

Frequently Asked Questions

Often providing a set of the most commonly asked questions
and accurate answers on a separate page of your website
before showing your customers contact information will
result in both the customer being satisfied and fewer contacts

for your agents. Frequently asked questions (FAQs) need to be kept current, and worded broadly enough so that your customers can quickly identify the question that best relates to their enquiry. Place your FAQs in a prominent position on help pages and display them above the option for customers to contact your team. An internet search will give you many pre-packaged options for your business. Most are reasonably priced and provide a simple and effective user interface.

Email Support

Most websites will offer email support as standard. Email can be effective as it provides customers with a written history of their interaction with your customer service team. Emails can also provide links to additional information, orders, postage tracking systems and a range of other aspects of your site that buyers might find useful. Most websites also use cut-and-paste responses to their customers' enquiries. From a cost and efficiency point of view, this of course saves your business quite a lot, but for the customer experience it can mean a response that sounds impersonal and sometimes inaccurate.

If using a system that employs cut-and-paste responses, ensure they have been professionally written by an online copywriter and train your agents in how to insert the information into an email template that allows 'topping and tailing', that is, individual content from your agents at the beginning and end of the message.

Ensure emails are well branded and clearly structured. Avoid excessive text and too many links pointing to other pages on your site. A customer is generally looking for a concise and effective response to their enquiry. Emails often have a lower first-contact resolution rate than other support methods due to their cut-and-paste answers. Customers will tend to respond to unsatisfactory emails to continue the thread of conversation. Wherever possible, establish an email contact system that returns responses to the same agent and avoid systems that do not allow buyers to respond at all.

Email support technology ranges from the very basic to the highly sophisticated and cost will vary depending on which way you choose to go.

Homework:

Use the email support at three websites and make a note of what system they are using. How efficient were responses? Were your issues resolved in the first contact? Make a list of functions that you would like your email system to include and conduct an internet search to assess what is available.

Comprehensive Help

Depending on the complexity of your website, or the range of products or services offered, you may also need to include a comprehensive help database which allows your customers to find information themselves. Most of these are keyword search based. Rather than build one yourself, Google offers websites the ability to upload code that allows customers to conduct a Google search within your own website. More information can be found at www.google.com/cse/.

In-person Customer Care

If you offer your customers the option of picking up goods, or provide a service that requires face-to-face customer interaction, make sure that your staff have been trained in the basics of customer interaction. You can have the best website in the world, but if customers do not enjoy interacting with your staff, the likely outcome is that you will lose customers rapidly. If offering pick-up, make sure your online purchases are stored in a separate area of your business so staff can quickly access them. Also ensure that your staff members know when to expect customers, and who has purchased online. Personalised service is a nice touch at the end of the impersonal purchase experience that online often provides.

CHAPTER SUMMARY

- You understand why online customers require a different kind of service from face-to-face customers

- You know the critical elements of online support success – what your system needs to have as a minimum

- You know the various options for online customer support and have assessed which one(s) would be most appropriate for your business

- You understand that customer service is a critical component of your business's success

- You understand the importance of training staff comprehensively, and ensuring each of your customer service agents feels like a valued and important part of your business

Interview with Paul Greenberg
Executive Chairman, DealsDirect Group

How are online customers different from offline ones?
Are their expectations any different?

Increasingly, I am of the view that 'retail is retail', whether offline or online. And retail has always had two key founding principles; 'Retail is detail', and 'the customer is always king'.

I think online retail has had a bit of a performance 'holiday' over the last few years as it has been a new channel. That is changing quickly. Customers increasingly have higher expectations across all channels, and the online customer, at the core, is no different.

How much of an investment should a business make
in the customer service offering (people, technology,
systems etc.)?

Customer service is the new differentiator, across all channels. A great customer experience is going to be crucial to ensure retail brands prosper. Social media is the catalyst that can build or grow a brand, or ultimately break it.

Customers are where they should be; in control! And investment in a quality customer experience across all touch points is not optional. It is mission critical.

What advice do you have for a business that wants to get online, but does not have experience in customer service?

Customer service is often very practical and logical. Start by asking the perennial question – What would I want as a customer? And remember that customers are patient and supportive as long as they are not being bullsh∗tted or ignored. Communicate, communicate, communicate!

What early mistakes did you make in your customer service, and how did you learn from those?

In the early days of eCommerce many of us thought that customer service online was a self-directed, 'self-serve' model. In many ways it is, but that does not mean that we should abdicate our responsibility to be there for our customers every step of the way. We have moderated this early view of self-service to self-service with support through all steps of the transaction.

Is the customer always right?

Absolutely. Even when they are not!

10
Putting It All Together

Your prioritised eCommerce action plan

WHAT THIS CHAPTER WILL COVER

- How to apply all that you have learnt throughout this book as a step-by-step, prioritised action plan for creating an effective long-term eCommerce strategy that will help grow your business

---

One Size Doesn't Fit All

There is a *lot* to learn when it comes to creating an effective long-term eCommerce strategy for your business. No one knows your business as well as you do and only you can make the decision that will decide the fate of your long-term business health. Throughout this book, I've covered a long list of options for you to consider as part of your eCommerce strategy and now I will pull them together into an example of a prioritised action plan for your business. Not all components of the plan will be applicable for your business or

209

you might have already completed some of the steps, so skip over those that do not apply. Consult with your business advisor, accountant and solicitor to make sure that you have all of your bases covered and are abiding by relevant laws in your area.

Month One

1. Size up the competition. Do your research thoroughly so you know exactly what kind of online presence your competitors have. You should be aware not only of the types of products they are selling online, but also which channels they are using and whether they are using them effectively. Just by looking at your competitors objectively, you should be able to put together a long list of actions to implement for your eCommerce strategy – both what to do, and what *not* to do. Buy from a range of your competitors so you can also assess the kind of service and overall experience they are offering, and understand what it would take to be better than them. Shop from both your local and international competitors.

2. Start thinking about your website and keep a running list of the must-have and the nice-to-have features to include. Mock up pages using pen and paper so it is clear in your mind.

3. If you have any excess inventory, or the ability to discount your goods or services, use a third party group

buy, deals or coupon site to set an expectation of the kind of volume you may sell online.

4. Complete your logistics research. By the end of month one, you should have identified the most cost-effective storage, packing and distribution options for your business.

Months Two to Three

1. Have your logistics ready to fulfil orders.
2. List your products on the online marketplace/s that is/ are most suitable for your business.
3. Identify the website designer or agency you want to work with and begin briefing your design ideas after chatting to some of their other clients.
4. Use your marketplace sales to help refine your business model. Are your logistics systems coping? Is your customer service satisfying buyer questions and exceeding buyer expectations?

Month Four

1. Your website will now be designed and tested. It will be live though you might not be directing a lot of traffic to it until you are confident that it is operating highly efficiently.
2. Participate in a marketplace's sale or deal program to drive incremental traffic to your store. Ensure your logistics and staff can cope with increased volumes.

3. Use social media to announce the launch of your website. Even if you don't have a website your customers are probably looking for you online, or your products or services, right now. You can start building your web presence before launching your actual website by reaching out to your customers via social media sites.

4. Use marketplace data to understand what is driving the bulk of your sales – what kinds of items, at what prices, and to what kind of buyers. Revisit your stock levels and range of supply to align with your key customer demographic.

Month Five

1. Drive more traffic to your website by buzz through social media and offline marketing, for example, create an introductory offer for a limited time. Your website URL should now be synonymous with your business name.

2. By the end of the month, ensure your site is performing well in SEO.

3. Use data to tweak your website's performance.

Month Six

1. Create a three-month test campaign for SEM. Measure which search engine, advertising campaign, affiliate or shopping comparison site is driving the best sell-through rate (as measured by sales divided by clicks).

2. Continually consult your data to ensure you are familiar with all success drivers of your online business and if a particular component is underperforming, try to improve it through optimisation, or else remove it from your strategy altogether.

Months Seven and Eight

1. Expand your channels to include more online marketplaces (including some international ones). Measure which ones give you the most sales per investment. You should know the percentage cost of the fees for each marketplace, but also additional costs of sale like time taken to communicate with buyers and fulfil orders, settle disputes, etc.

2. You will now be using social media to communicate about new product lines and exciting developments within your website or industry, and to learn more about your customers and their experience of your products or services.

3. By the end of month eight you will have calculated a precise ROI for all channels you have trialled including marketplaces and SEM. Now you have a prioritised list of channels to employ, and will assign your budget accordingly. When there is more budget, you will utilise more channels, when there is less, you will concentrate on the top few.

Month Nine

1. By now, you will be doing everything in your power to drive as much traffic to your website as possible. You will have created a finely tuned eCommerce strategy that is optimised for traffic, converting traffic to sales and providing your business with the highest ROI since you first launched your eCommerce strategy nine months ago.

The Future

1. You and your staff will remain on top of eCommerce and mobile commerce developments to ensure your business is at the cutting edge of trends and technology.
2. Your website will be updated accordingly, at least every 18 months but ideally every six months.
3. You will join a number of internet industry bodies or associations to help you maintain your knowledge and contacts.

Your Expanded Business

It all sounds rather simple when you put it into a nine-month plan like this, doesn't it? The reality is that the implementation of your eCommerce strategy will be an evolving project and will take you considerable time, energy and financial resources. If you are an existing business, the cost of creating an efficient transactional website would be akin to opening a new bricks-and-mortar store. Think of all the costs involved, from design and fit-out, to staff, training, stock and marketing all before you open the doors, then the ongoing costs of rent, wages, more marketing . . . the list goes on.

You should view your website as a considerable expansion of your business, but one with a different cost structure and a whole new way of operating. Only those businesses that invest sufficiently (time, money and knowledge) are currently reaping the rewards that online can bring. The businesses that think having a website is a simple matter of tacking it onto a small corner of their operation will quickly learn that an online presence requires considerably more focus and energy. Your success is largely dictated by the amount you outlay but, conversely, paying more than anyone else to launch an eCommerce channel for your business does not guarantee success. The beauty of online is that nearly everything is measurable because data is readily available and the astute online operator is one who pays close attention to what the data is saying, and adjusts their business quickly to capitalise on growth trends.

Finally . . .

An effective online strategy will grow your business

Any Australian business that does not have an online strategy has limited its potential for growth. Your customers are online now, and most of them are looking for your business, products or services online, too. If you do not have a website that contains your entire inventory and that is fully transactional, you will be losing sales to your competitors. Online commerce is growing much faster than traditional retail and, as technology evolves, more customers will prefer the online shopping experience to the offline one. Developments in mobile will blur the lines between online and offline so even if after reading this book you don't think you need a website, by the end of next year more customers will be finding you via online and mobile than any other way.

Throughout this book, I have provided a wide range of information designed to help you create a tailored eCommerce strategy for your business. Consultants could charge you tens of thousands of dollars to create an eCommerce strategy but everything you need is out there, and easy to find if you know where to look without having to spend nearly as much as that. You have the power and ability to get online, right now.

Having a successful website that will grow your customer base and increase sales requires you to consider a wide range of often complex and technical solutions. Not every option will be appropriate for your business, and it is unlikely that you will have the best eCommerce strategy possible from day one of your website's launch. Evolve your strategy as your customers react to the various components and always ensure you refer to the data that online provides – it will quickly highlight those aspects of your strategy that are not performing well or driving a profitable return on investment.

Speak to your colleagues, friends and work associates to get ideas for what has worked well for them. There is no one-size-fits-all eCommerce strategy but every business can learn from others. Allocate one hour of each week to teach yourself something new about eCommerce and take that knowledge to refine your strategy and deliver the best possible experience for your customers. This will involve buying from your competitors both locally and internationally, conducting research on new technologies, and following trends and the most popular eCommerce developments around the globe.

In summary, there are five tips that are non-negotiable for your business's eCommerce strategy:

1. Online marketplaces will allow you to get your products online in a matter of hours, without you

having to have your own website. The most popular marketplaces have an abundance of shoppers looking for your products, right now.

2. Build your own website now. Include your entire range of products or services and make it fully transactional.

3. Ensure you have the best possible logistics solution in place for your website.

4. Drive traffic to your site for free using SEO (natural search) and a highly optimised mix of paid online advertising and marketing.

5. Your website address should be synonymous with your business name – wherever a customer sees one, they see the other.

You may not see results from your eCommerce strategy on day one but the best strategies are built for ongoing success, and not to capitalise on the current trend or fad. In five years' time you will wonder how you ever thought it was possible for your business to survive without being fully transactional online.

Helpful Resources

The internet itself can be your best resource for finding out more information about creating a successful online strategy. Be smart in the way you search for information, and look beyond the first two pages of results. Look for Australia-specific information so you can adopt local practices but keep in mind that international trends, particularly in the US, are often a sign of what is to come. Here are some resources that may help you refine your eCommerce strategy:

- **Techcrunch** (www.techcrunch.com) is a source of great articles, latest news and industry insight. Subscribe to receive daily alerts.
- **Mumbrella** (www.mumbrella.com.au) is an enewsletter worth signing up for. It will keep you up to date on trends, news and the movements of key marketing industry figures with a particular slant toward online.
- *Selling Online: How to Become a Successful eCommerce Merchant* by Jim Carroll and Rick Broadhead, though US-centric and slightly outdated, is a solid reference book.
- *How to Use eBay & PayPal* and *How to Make Money on eBay* both by Todd Alexander, are online-marketplace specific but include numerous tips that can be applied to both your marketplace and broader eCommerce strategies.
- *Nett* magazine often contains helpful articles, and tips and advice for creating a more effective website as well as industry news and developments.
- Explore Google more fully – among its pages you will find a wealth of information, data and tips for successful eCommerce.

Associations and Events

- Online Retailers Event (ORE) is run annually and features a range of speakers and knowledgeable delegates and sponsors. More information can be found at www.onlineretailer.net.
- PeSA is the Professional eBay Sellers Alliance (www.gopesa.org) and is an association for like-minded e-tailers to share best practice and advice. It hosts a yearly summit.

Endnotes

1   Forrester Research is a global research company that releases regular reports on the size of Australian eCommerce. For Australian forecast figures to 2015, refer to www.forrester.com

2   http://www.comscore.com/Press_Events/Press_ Releases/2010/1/Global_Search_Market_Grows_46_ Percent_in_2009; Assumptions = Based on Dec 09 US data, 30% CAGR, AU = 20% of US market, Dec = 12.5% of yearly activity.

3   Telsyte: www.telsyte.com.au; 'Business confidence in group buying strong amid high campaign satisfaction.'

4   'Stop the Hate: Daily Deals Aren't All Bad, And Here's Why' by Arash Pirzad-Allaei; http:// techcrunch.com/2011/06/25/stop-the-hate-daily-deals-arent-all-bad-and-heres-why/

5   The Australia Institute, 'The Rise and Rise of Online Retail' can be found at www.tai.org.au

6   http://www.theage.com.au/small-business/more-gasps-as-shop-service-spat-spreads-20110930-1l07x.html

7   The Australia Institute, 'The Rise and Rise of Online Retail' can be found at www.tai.org.au

Acknowledgements

Bernadette Foley for your immediate support of this project, and being a long-term believer in my work.

Deb Sharkey for giving me an incredible opportunity to balance two things I love.

Dan Feiler for the advice, coaching and information sharing.

The industry experts who gave their time in providing advice and information for this book: Deb Sharkey, Frerk-Malte Feller, Adam Shalagin, Anthony Sukow, Simon Smith, Jethro Marks, Paul Greenberg, Ming Foong, Grace Chu.

Thank you to David Koch and Jenny Dobbin.

Colleagues, friends and peers whose knowledge contributed to the content of this book: Cheryl Akle, Duncan Brett, Adam Canter, Belinda Chiarella, Brian Cottrell, Melanie Dudgeon, Jochen Eckert, Jake Henrich, Jo Hicks, Mark Lancaster, Andrew Lasky, Nicolette Maury, Hamish Moline, David Odgers, Oliver Rees, Jeff Ross, Greg Schneider, Scott Shillinglaw, Hamish Stone, Lisa Wong, Noah Zamansky … and everyone at the eBay Inc family.

A huge thank you to the many, many eBay sellers I have met over the past ten years for sharing your stories and insights.

And Jibz, thanks for understanding that spending long days with nothing but a keyboard for company can sometimes impact my ability to speak...temporarily.

About the Author

Todd Alexander has been working in retail and online for twenty years. Currently the Director of Selling at eBay, over the past ten years Todd has appeared at numerous summits and conferences dedicated to helping businesses successfully get online.

His novel, *Pictures of Us* (Hachette Australia), was published in 2006. His second book, *How to Buy and Sell on eBay. com.au: The Official Pocket Guide* (Hachette Australia), has sold in excess of 40 000 copies. In 2010, an advanced guide to eBay, *How to Make Money on eBay*, was published by Allen & Unwin, followed in 2011 by *How to Use eBay and PayPal* (Hachette Australia).

Todd manages a successful online business of his own and lives in Sydney. A graduate of Macquarie University, he has degrees in Modern Literature and Law.

www.toddalexander.net.au
http://gybo.com.au/
Twitter: @Todd_Alexander

Index